WHY?...B'CUZ

##############

Sherwood Goozée

Published by
Truth Seeker Company
239 S. Juniper Street
Escondido, California 92025
www.truthseeker.com

ISBN# 0-939040-48-3

65

In memory of my parents,
Alan and Zala

Dedicated to "The Professor"
and you, the reader

Foreword

One of the most gratifying aspects of this book is that the author does not address us with the fervor of religionists or atheists (such as I am). He is at pains to be reasonable, undogmatic, questioning. He does not allow certainty and surmise to become entwined. His acumen is mildly projected and his decency both obvious and uplifting. In his dissertation, he reminds me slightly of the meticulousness of John Ruskin who once declared: "I am never satisfied that I have handled a subject properly till I have contradicted myself at least three times."

It has been said that superstitions [from the Latin *superstes* = that which survives] are religious forms surviving the loss of ideas. It may also be said that religion is an instrument for harnessing superstition in order to impose some degree of control and symmetry upon peoples. Such an exercise sometimes works and sometimes doesn't; sometimes inspirits and sometimes corrupts. As early as a generation before Rome was burnt by the Gauls, it was remarked (according to Livy) that foreign religion had invaded the city, brought by prophets who made money out of the superstitions they roused and the alien and unusual means they employed to procure the peace of the gods: the sacrifice of goats and young dogs, and of sacred cakes the Vestals made from the first ears of the last year's harvest. The celebrants smeared blood on their brows and wore the skins of the slaughtered goats. This Feast of Lupercal continued into A.D. the fifth century when it was merely replaced by Pope Gelasius with a Christian event of similar melodrama. Thereafter, revelers smeared their brows with soot (Ash Wednesday) and focused on one divinity instead of several.

Modern Deism is hard to measure. A Jewish acquaintance of mine, an Oxford graduate of formidable intellectual achievement, mentioned recently that he considered himself to be a Deist, but seldom mentioned this to acquaintances, "Lest they misunderstand." I suspect few Deists proclaim themselves as such simply because proclaiming anything seems a touch religious in these disturbing times when religious fanaticism is often perceived as a threat to democracy, if not to civilization itself.

Yet as a belief, proclaimed or not, Deism has been a quiet nudge in civilization's ribs for quite some time. The Roman Horace was privately as secular-minded as his odes were occasionally religious promotions. He laughed at superstition and ridiculed the idea of a divine interest in men. Significantly, perhaps, Horace's candor, his humor, his amiability, combines to give him a very human charm, even as his religious compeers regarded his "spiritual" side as sterile and insufficient.

Life has been crowded down the ages with cult and ritual and usage, full of divinities, petty, pleasing or grotesque, but generally vague and ill-defined. Dragon's tongue, eyes and gall were once prescribed by the Magi for those who are "harassed by gods of the night and by Fauns", who caused "panic" fears. Pliny said that trees were "temples of the divinities", and country people until fairly recently would hang rags and other offerings, including walking-sticks and crutches following "miraculous" cures, on their branches (I witnessed this myself a few years ago at the church of Sainte Anne de Beaupre in Quebec). Holy wells are as common in Ireland as they were in ancient Rome. Superstition or, to give it its "respectable" terminology, religion, has interfered with diet for centuries. For example, Jews would not "eat with blood", lest the soul of the beast should pass into man.

Yet we should not feel superior today. Virtually

every national or international event now, in part, resembles a parody of religious celebration. Spectators weep and abase themselves at sporting events. The election of an American President lacks only a puff of white smoke to rival the appointment of a new Pope. I have long worried about what I see as intermittent, though increasingly frequent occurrences of, secular hysteria, in that, *inter alia*, it seems to mimic, and in many cases, replaces religiosity, especially its more extreme manifestations. Religion and ersatz religion have subverted humanity, just as they are seeking to undermine the evolution of species theory. We seem to have fallen under the spell of nut-cases. Goozee is right when he says: "We're being programmed not to think for ourselves." Which means we have no self-knowledge. And even should some of us seek to understand the nonphysical truths that affect us, "definitive answers are elusive."

Thinking for oneself does not, automatically, lead one to Deism. But it sets one on the road to personal discovery, logical deduction, release from propagation of pious nonsense and other attainments that may finally drop you there. Whether it leads humanity to moral progress is, I suppose, arguable. Sherwood Goozee argues it adroitly, and often convincingly. On the other hand, I cannot help but recall Horace's response to a man who boasts   of moral progress and his freedom from avarice. OK, says Horace, but...

"You're not a miser. Good - but prithee
say,
Is every vice with avarice flown away? ...
Does Superstition ne'er tour heart assail
Nor bid your soul with fancied horrors
quail?
Or can you smile at magic's strange
alarms,
Dreams, witchcraft, ghosts, Thessalian
spells and charms?"

Cal McCrystal

Holy Molie

God helps those who help themselves...
Horatio Alger, 1865

Let me set the stage for this semi irreverent magnum opus blockbuster of a book that was three years in the making. First of all a confession, how appropriate for someone presuming to write about life and the God phenomenon, I am not a writer by trade nor an expert of any sort, and I may as well admit it now because I'm sure it will reveal itself at some point later on. (no, that's not why it took so long.) I'm just an ordinary person, such as yourself, but one who has had the luxury of time to think about our existence and to come up with some answers that may surprise you...they did me. This is my first and only book and is in fact an extension of a paper that I authored several years earlier for my own edification...*IZ Sense*.

When you know something of my life, it may help to connect the dots later on. A little background music, please. The youngest son of a protestant

11

minister, I spent most of my early life in Napa, California, where for eleven years my father was pastor of the Methodist church. He was a liberal person and because of experiences in his own life, he never imposed his beliefs on either my brother or myself; he recognized that we should be the ones to make decisions for ourselves on the subject of faith...thank goodness. However, church as well as church related activities played a central role in our family and social life. For my part, I never questioned the teachings of the church...just accepted everything as the way things should be...not strongly believing or disbelieving and enjoying the nonchalance of youth along the way. Had it been otherwise and I hadn't been so unconcerned, my life might have been quite different.

Though I never thought too much about the church services themselves, I always wondered if the parishioners truly believed what they were saying as they recited the liturgy, sang the songs, and prayed the prayers...because "for mine own part, 'twas Greek to me". I always thought a pop-quiz should have been given to see how many got the points my Dad had made or if they really understood what they were saying and singing. What does, "...power in the blood of the lamb, wonder working power...." from the old gospel hymn mean? Not only could I not make head nor tail of much of what I heard, I never bothered to find out what it all meant. I don't think I took life very seriously...even though World War II was raging.

In 1945 after graduating from high school at seventeen, I left home and, as might be expected being raised in a small town, was a little scared when admitted to the United States Merchant Marine Academy. After almost "two years before the mast" on a queasy stomach and seasick most of the time, life in the academy was not an extremely happy experience. No wonder after basic training and a year at sea; I resigned my midshipman status because the briny was obviously not for me. While in college, being more clown than academic, I found myself in the theater with hopes of becoming an actor. When the Korean conflict began, I enlisted in the naval reserve so as to graduate from college and avoid the draft. I remained in school an extra year to earn a teaching credential as well, not because I really wanted to teach but to please my parents, who had always been more than good to me; however, when school was over, duty called. Fortunately, I was stationed on Guam rather than aboard ship to become a radio announcer for Armed Forces Radio Service, and later start a theater at the naval base before being discharged.

In sequence, after "serving" my country came the professional theater in New York, two lovely daughters, an unfortunate and unhappy marriage of twenty-one plus years, a divorce, twenty-nine years of teaching, and finally, four years before retiring, at the young age of fifty-seven, praise be to Allah, a happy marriage to a soul mate.

Theater had always been a labor of love, but only the fortunate few get to wed their first love...the rest of us mesh the ideal and the real into an uneasy compromise, and so it was with me. After leaving the theater for family reasons, I can't say that my life really had a great deal of direction other than to try and stay afloat. It wasn't as if I were doing what I wanted to do...like a doctor or lawyer might or anyone who felt a real calling. I had no particular ambitions to pursue...just bills that had to be paid. Sometimes working two or three jobs at a time while teaching, my days were spent attempting to make ends meet and grasping for survival strategies in an unhappy marriage to a wife with emotional problems. At that time, I didn't know whether I was Christian, agnostic, or atheist, and not much time was spent thinking about it one way or the other...no ideology was going to change my unfortunate circumstances.

Fast forward a number of years to a wonderful new spouse, a new life, and a smile on my face that only a happy marriage can bring as retirement beckoned. When it finally happened, I was extremely content to be living on our isolated ranch of forty acres with not a care in the world. I couldn't have wanted more.

Soon there was a new century, and a few years after that a surge from the Christian right into national politics. That was what did it for me! That's what awakened me from a state of mental apathy. I felt that the Christian religion of my father was being hi-jacked by a group of pulpit-pounding zealots who were using religion to enrich themselves while politicians manipulated their parishioners to gain votes and inject religion into my government. How dare they! The more I saw of what was happening the angrier I got, even though by this time I considered myself an atheist. The Christian right had no right to impose their beliefs on the nation. **HOLY COW!** What happened to separation of church and state? Then I thought, if I'm so intensely against their beliefs, what am I for? Why was I an atheist? Was it because it was the easy thing to do, to "just say no" and not think about it? It seemed only fair that I should find some answers for myself to these perplexing questions.

Having always been a do-it-yourselfer by necessity, I reasoned that if I was going to complain, I should be able to come up with a better idea or else stop complaining. For the first time in my life, I decided to try and make sense of human existence by clearing my mind of all preconceived ideas and starting from scratch to find answers to questions that had previously been avoided. Over the course of several years, my thoughts gradually took shape, and I eventually wrote what I believed to be true about life...editing and re-editing until I was finally satisfied with the results.   It ended up as a terse sixteen-page essay, and to my great surprise a belief in God, though not the Christian God of Abraham. Friends who read the paper gave it favorable reviews. Some even wanted copies and thanked me for expressing what they were unable to put into words**.   HOLY MACKEREL!** How about that!

Several months later I purchased a number of CD's from The Teaching Company, which records and produces lectures by the best professors in their field on a wide variety of topics. At the time I was listening to "The Great Ideas of Philosophy, 2nd Edition" which was a superb sixty-lecture course given by Daniel N. Robinson, Philosophy Professor at Oxford University and Distinguished Professor Emeritus, Georgetown University, who had written or edited over 40 books. Needless to say, I was very impressed by his lectures; I'd never heard anything quite like it before. As the course proceeded I began to realize that some of the things he was talking about were actually in my paper...a little Decartes maybe, a dash of Sarte, possibly some Kierkegaard, and definitely a sprinkling of William James. What nerve!! They had taken my ideas...OK, so it was years before I'd thought of it, and yes, their ideas were developed in somewhat more detail...like books, but **HOLY TOLEDO**, I got my rights!! Actually, it gave me a very nice feeling...my essay made sense after all.

Being rather brash, you might say "ballsy" for an octogenarian, I decided to send my paper to "The Professor". I found his Oxford University email address on the Internet and sent my essay off wondering what his impression would be, though never in my wildest dreams expecting a reply...well, maybe my wildest. And then I opened my email one day and there it was right in front of my eyes...busy as he was, he even thanked me for writing to him, wow, and referring to my paper he said "...thoughts with which I find myself strongly concurring." **WOW!!** I'd hit the jackpot! I wasn't so crazy, after all. Then in a subsequent email he said, "I strongly encourage you to print the essay and to distribute it as broadly as your resources permit....", and he even recommended some journals that might be interested in publishing it.

Now, I was in a pickle...he expected me to do something about this. And so it was that I began printing copies of my paper and sending them off to various personages, expecting them to get as excited as I was. Didn't happen...although Bill Moyers replied and said he had read it twice and "...found it quite provocative and engaging". Not bad, not bad! The Dalai Lama's secretary acknowledged receiving it and said thanks. Paris Hilton sent me her photograph. Not great, but **HOLY MOLIE**, not bad. If you'd like to read the essay you can find it at "religioustolerance.com" which graciously published it as a guest editorial.

The next surprise came when by chance I Googled the word "Deism". As I read the definition, I realized that in large part that was what my essay was about. **HOLY _ _ _ _!! I'M A DEIST!!** I wasn't alone after all! I was a Deist and lots of people thought as I did...Voltaire, Einstein, Thomas Paine, Thomas Jefferson to mention a few...and all those Freethinkers, too...perhaps not exactly as I thought, after all we are each individuals created from a variety of experiences and needs, still there is a truth that we each recognize. Acknowledging my new insight, albeit via the back door, demanded some inclusions and minor revisions to the *IZ sense* paper on life and the God phenomenon that I had written earlier. What follows is a personal awakening that culminated in Deism. I've tried to view the God phenomenon of Deism in the broad perspective of our existence rather than a narrower context of competing ideologies.

Real Revelations

The nature of God is a circle, of which the center is everywhere and the circumference is nowhere.
                                    --Empedocles, c. 450 BC.

So who am I writing this therapeutic adventure for besides myself? Oddly enough, I consider it my gift to you, the reader. It's really all that I have to give, and you may or may not find it useful, though of course, I hope that you do…that remains to be seen. My only expertise is that "I've been there, done that"…I mean life. Yes, I'm old, perhaps ancient by your standards, but I have had some experiences and thoughts that in many ways surprised me, and I'd like to share a few of them with you. For those of you who are young, consider it a fairly reliable chart from one sailor to another to navigate the long voyage ahead…a treacherous journey for the ill prepared into the unknown, and for "ancient mariners" such as myself lying at anchor, a debatable reminiscence of how we weathered the storms. Not that I wish to tell you how to live your life, but wouldn't it be a good idea to know something of what to expect in the future as well as the order of things…because, you know, there is an order even in what appears to be chaos.

These observations come primarily from personal experiences…some good, some bad and many hours of contemplating life, which most people don't have the time to do or perhaps the inclination, but if you haven't tried it, it's a rewarding exercise I highly recommend. The subject matter is something seldom discussed in our society; I don't think it's taught in school, yet it's something that I wish I had known at an earlier age. If you like, consider it that chat with Mom or Dad that you never had but later wished you did.

Today, life races on at a hectic pace bombarding us with so much stuff and more stuff that it's hard to make sense of anything. Every new gadget comes with an instruction manual that almost requires a college degree to understand…nothing is simple. In large metropolitan areas, where most people live, children are programmed for school and for play whether they like it or not; either that, or all too often, they are left to fend for themselves in a dangerous world by parents trying to keep their heads above water with little time to reflect on the consequences of what is happening around them.

Like an army of ants we rush, rush, rush to get it all done. And just what is the "it" that is so important? Are we afraid to stop and contemplate life for fear we may find only emptiness? So we fill the void with speakers, human and electric, let the TV blare...god forbid we should have some quiet time or we should seriously communicate with one another...put on the headphones, crank up the volume, play the music and let the noise continue. Live the lies by whatever means possible and don't let the treadmill stop; otherwise, we might not know what to do. Just STOP! We're being programmed not to think for ourselves, and to all this I say **GET A LIFE!** There's more to living than being a wired automaton with a Visa card...but where do we begin?

When I worked in the theater as a young man, I learned a very important lesson about acting that also applies to life...one that hopefully you may already have learned. I discovered that if a character in a play is to be portrayed successfully, it's essential for the actor to know the character's theme or purpose. Why is the character in the play, what does he want...not in generalities such as happiness or love but specifically...what would make him happy or what could he do to merit love? Without having these kinds of answers, the portrayal as well as the play go nowhere disintegrating before the audience's eyes, making it a waste of everyone's time and an unpleasant experience for the actor involved. Purposeful direction and understanding of each character is essential to the play's overall success. With that critical insight, one has a sense of how to proceed, making success more likely. The same may be said of life as well. What is our goal in life? What are we trying to accomplish? The decision is ours to make, of course, and once made we can act and react confidently by making choices that achieve our goal.

Meanwhile, each day our thoughts and actions are creating a unique special person, and we define that person in many ways: by the clothes we wear, the music we like, the people we befriend, the entertainments we enjoy, the books we read or don't read, the responses we make, and the language we use, for example. These outward manifestations reflect the inner person...rather like looking in a mirror. But does it reflect the kind of person we want to create, and how can we alter our behavior to mold a person to our liking? That ability requires self-knowledge, knowledge about how the world operates, and what the effects of choice are. Not knowing these parameters may result in an unhappy outcome. If you haven't thought about it before, think about it now...be prepared to question conventional wisdom and to challenge your ideas.

I shall never forget the little boy that I met when I was a teenager. What a pest he was. He must have been about three or four years old, and he never stopped asking me the question, "Why?" Regardless of what my answer was, he would always respond with why. It was so frustrating that I eventually said, "Because...that's why," thinking that it would put a stop to his incessant questions. However, nothing could deter him and again he would say, "Why?" It seemed as if it was the only word he knew.

Thinking back on it, I now see it in a different context because asking why is what mankind does and has been doing since the beginning of time. Nowadays, we continue to ask why until we reach a plausible answer. That's really what science is all about, but eons ago if answers weren't forthcoming, we were likely to conclude that it was some kind of supernatural phenomenon. Whence came mysticism, superstition, and lots and lots of "gods". Eventually, once reason failed, the shamans and priests of religion were there to fill in the gaps...but more of that later.

First of all, I think scientists will agree that among life's universal operating principles are the principles of interdependency and life cycle. Both material and abstract elements, including plant and animal life, are interdependent. Like a self-contained organism each component is dependent upon the next. We are literally family in every respect whether we like it or not, and it's beneficial if we accept the fact. Secondly, the cycle of life is a continuum of birth, struggle and death, rebirth, struggle and death *ad infinitum*. This process is as true for molecular biology as it is for the cosmos and us. We may have little control over birth and death, but daily struggles are a different matter, and how we approach them is crucial to our happiness.

Rather than being safe, the universe is a hostile environment of varying scale…a world of constant change and flux in which each entity uses developed skills to survive. For reasons known and many unknown, challenges are thrust upon individuals and society while others we deliberately create for ourselves in commerce, entertainments, sciences, and the arts. These challenges never cease and are crucial to giving life meaning and gratification, but when they are unresolved, we despair and become frustrated. While personal challenges may differ in degree and nature from person to person, we each cope with their effects daily, and none are immune. In the midst of these daily trials attitude and effort are key to a successful conclusion.

From the point-of-view of mankind, the universe

functions on two fundamental levels—
NONPHYSICAL AND PHYSICAL: Nonphysical
with regard to utilization of nature's eternal laws
and nonphysical in selective choices of action that
ultimately define the extent of our humanity--
physical with respect to the tangible universe
around us which is forged by nonphysical natural
laws. Although the nonphysical has primacy over
the physical, they are co-dependent and interact
with one another. The material world could not
exist without the controlling laws of nature. This
being said, many universal truths of the
nonphysical and physical world are yet to be
discovered or understood, and we must remain
open to the inevitability of change dismantling
outdated concepts in favor of new reasoned
revelations as they arise...even to the extent of
God's existence. The puzzle never ends.

Least understood and most difficult to unravel are
the nonphysical truths that affect each of us.
Although study of the mind and human
psychology has finally been given the emphasis it
deserves, controversy is still intense. Definitive
answers are elusive, and, as stated earlier,
whatever is postulated here is subject to change as
new knowledge unfolds. With this in mind, self-
examination becomes even more important since
the way we see ourselves in large part determines
our chances for success and happiness.

When we live by myths, life can be a very dangerous existence. Consider "ignorance is bliss" or "what you don't know won't hurt you", for example. Myths are a two-sided coin giving myopic comfort on the one hand and blinding us from reality on the other; consequently, we are likely to miss options that could resolve problems. "America is the greatest nation on earth". "We have the best healthcare system in the world". These are nice catch phrases for politicians, but are the statements true or is it a way of avoiding the truth, and moreover, what is the criteria used for making such statements? Kinda smacks of "My Dad is better than your Dad", doesn't it?

Beneficial growth is difficult to achieve when we put our trust in myths alone. Truth is necessary to reach the goals that myths only imply. If we are to make progress, we must find truth and break the shackles of ignorance; fortunately, there are a large number of people engaged in this effort. One such organization is The Templeton Foundation, which gives large grants of money to investigate a wide range of areas that have impact on the human condition including the exploration of self. However, though we may not be experts, there are many observations that all are capable of noting without a great amount of expertise, and what follows is the pursuit of a few.

From the moment seeds leave the pod or sperm navigate to egg, the struggle to succeed has begun. Like a computer chip, miraculously every living thing in the universe is individually given the information necessary to reach its potential. It's not a time for "I give up" or "I don't care". That may come later after feeling the lash of broken promises, despair, and hopelessness, but at the beginning of the race, regardless of our gene pool, we all strive by whatever means to maximize our potential. That potential may be defined and measured individually for a thoughtful few utilizing nonphysical truths or by cultures that instill superficial perceptions of achievement. Most notably, money and power. True, success is often rewarded in this manner, but is this popular definition always valid? Is the old saying "winning beats whatever's second" really true? For example, does winning by cheating and lying or luck really give inner gratification or just a shallow outward display of satisfaction and fear of the next hurdle to be encountered? I think we know the answer to that.

It's difficult not to notice the duality often found in life…physical and nonphysical, proton and neutron, love and hate, positive force countered by negative force. For instance, one cannot know happiness without having been sad at some time, and the same contrasting dualistic relationship can be said for all emotions. Every positive emotion has a counterpart negative emotion. Action is usually the catalyst, emotion is the response; therefore, choice of action is intricately involved exposing others and us to a variety of feelings...often very deeply. Naturally, whenever possible, positive choice is the best choice of action because it usually creates positive emotions while negativism elicits negative emotions. By doing a hateful thing, you're likely get to hate back...don't you think? Fortunately, human beings have an innate desire for happiness, another nonphysical law of nature; therefore, it is in our own best interest and the interest of others to be positive.

Contentment is a neutral condition that most of us seek...a soothing equilibrium...the coda of our musical piece. How can we achieve it? If you haven't heard otherwise by now, we are naturally lazy. We work hard at discovering efficiencies to save us from work; we hire others to work for us. Moreover, we seem to require a stimulus to provoke us into whatever work we can't get out of...hence wives (I'm joking, please, I'm joking). When an impetus exists, it is usually caused by internal desires...for example, hunger and sex are both strong activators, or by external causation such as the elements or other external force. To illustrate my point in another way, we wouldn't close the window unless we felt cold...though our preference is to be undisturbed. Nothing is more natural than to seek resolution of situations so that we can return to a state of contented equilibrium...rather like a pendulum coming to rest. Observe it in art, mathematics, nature, or more simply, watch someone adjust a skewed picture on the wall. Order and balance are a natural state sought in our lives, and that characteristic stimulates us to grapple challenges of a chaotic world so that they can be resolved and we can return to an even keel.

Security is another universal need, and it manifests itself in many different ways. Naturally, food and shelter are a first priority, but the interrelationship of identity and a sense of belonging are also high on the list. We each would like to be recognized as someone special and important within the groups to which we ally ourselves. Our first group experience occurs within the family where we use various strategies to achieve recognition and acceptance. Outside the family we join groups that advocate mutual interests while some may join just to feel needed. Elite groups have stringent standards for acceptance, and others accept anyone who wishes to be one of them...often reaching for the lowest common denominator. Requirements for membership may include any one or a combination of things such as ideology, loyalty, intelligence, education, social status, money, ambition, appearance, behavior, or ethnicity. Belonging bolsters our sense of security and pride through identification with others, and depending on our initiative, most will sacrifice or work to achieve whatever memberships require. The exception is the outcast, the loner who doesn't trust any person or group and prefers self-reliance; outwardly, he wants no extended family or perhaps is unwilling to make whatever effort is required, yet paradoxically, yearns to be accepted. Another exception is the person who has a strong sense of purpose and becomes a leader to whom others are attracted. Inner motives for joining organizations are as varied as the members themselves, but security in numbers and identity are part of the equation.

Hope is a normal condition also. The most pessimistic pessimist has a glimmer of hope deep down inside; even the person committing suicide has hope that, if nothing else, the bullet doesn't miss its target. Since we all have this sense of hope, it means there is also the possibility of despair…and at worst, disaster. We try to lessen the odds of it happening to us in any number of ways both ethical and unethical, but still, sorry to say, no matter what we do life sometimes can be a crap-shoot…part of the built in struggle for survival. It's hard to watch pain and suffering of the innocent afflicted by disease or natural disasters. What have they done to deserve it? We hope that it doesn't happen to us or anyone we know, but it often does. We hope we remain healthy, we hope we don't have an accident. We hope we find the right mate and enjoy a useful, happy life, but it doesn't always work out that way. In some instances we have control over the matter, but in others we don't.

Fate seems to be part of life...nothing is a sure thing...no guarantees. Unpredictable mutated genes create new species or possibly sicken and mutilate existing species. In nature weak and infirmed animals die off in order to preserve and strengthen the species, but fortunately, mankind is blessed with a special compensation to nature's ravages. Hope and compassion are part of our character. People in the direst circumstances still hope that their fortunes will reverse, and it is our obligation to help those who through no fault of their own are distressed. Medical science is founded on compassion with the hope that suffering can be eased or eradicated. The extent of these uniquely human responses tests the measure of our humanity separating us from other species and represent nonphysical truths with which we are blessed.

Wanting to be right is part of our makeup, too. We

join causes and institutions because we think that they are right-minded...doing good for either ourselves or for society. The ultimate example of this desire to do "right" is enlistment in the military to fight for what one believes and if necessary, to lay down one's life...in the Iraq war Sergeant Tillman comes to mind, and I will never forget the look on the faces of West Point cadets as President Obama spoke to them about their mission to help the people of Afghanistan. It was clear that the cadets were eager to do what they perceived as right.

No one joins a group to do what they consider as "wrong". Even members of criminal gangs believe in what they do, albeit evil; they selfishly justify their actions as "right" for themselves and their family of cohorts. However, putting aside the warped minds of a few, the "right" that all can agree upon, teach, and try to follow is to do for others what we would want them to do for us. That is the universal definition of fairness found in all major religions. This is not religious dogma; this is a universal precept that people understand. It is the foundation of justice. The acid test for individuals and society alike lies in this definition and all should hold themselves accountable to it in personal and communal life. Adherence to it should undeniably be included in defining an admirable person. Does acting selfishly either individually or collectively in any way advance our cause over the long haul? Aren't there ramifications from negative behavior that affect us all? If as a people we are to be successful, we must break the bonds of selfish negativity that are at the root of human conflict. Positive creativity that exhibits fairness and equanimity is the ultimate solution...let it begin with each of us. The matter of right choice fundamentally enhances all lives, and surely "rightness", that is to say the effect of justice, should be considered when contemplating nonphysical laws of nature. It represents one of man's highest attributes and is an important part of fulfilling our potential.

Certainly, everyone would like a successful life...on the job and as a person. Though success means different things to different people, no one deliberately tries to be a failure. I think it is safe to say that no sane person gets up in the morning saying, "Today I'm going to wrong others or do a bad job because it will make me feel so good". What makes us feel good, what makes us feel successful, is doing things the right way. The problem of course is, "What is right?" For selfish people, right is whatever is good for them, and to hell with everyone else, but even selfish people instinctively would like to do what is right or at least put on the facade of what is right rather than face public scorn. Selfishness is a trait we all share, and often it gets in the way of our own best interests. Ironically, when that happens, cooperating with the other person may be the best solution for all concerned. Collaboration and teamwork lead to success more often than failure.

If we can recognize justice and seek it for ourselves, why is it that so many have a difficulty doing what is right? Undoubtedly, it must be a combination of many things including immaturity, repetitive unhappy experiences, and environment that over time have had a negative impact on our sensitivities. Sometimes we can't seem to help ourselves and don't know why we act as we do. Often, if we only knew why we behave the way we do, we wouldn't. So the first step is to try and find an answer to the "why". If self-analysis doesn't resolve the issue, remember that we are creatures of habit so repeated conscious efforts to overcome negativity may eventually lead to a positive outlook and a realization that whatever deep-seated fears we had were unwarranted.

Psycho-cybernetics is also a useful tool that can be incorporated to alter ones attitude and behavior. Athletes, musicians, and others use the process to help achieve a wanted outcome. This is the practice of using the mind's eye to visualize actions and results...a rehearsal of sorts that is repeated numerous times imaging a successful response to whatever it was we were trying to achieve. The baseball player visualizes the ball approaching the plate and his hitting the ball in perfect form. The violinist visualizes her fingers moving across the frets with perfect timing and hears the tone of each note played. You might say it is a pragmatic mantra...a practical prayer for success. With concentrated repetitive visualization of achieving our goal, the desired result is more likely to occur, and there is satisfaction in knowledge that regardless of the outcome by using this process you have in fact become the positive person you wanted to be.

How do we come to see ourselves the way we do, and what part does conscience play in the equation? Understanding the answer to this question has profound ramifications. Imagine if you will, two families, family "A" and family "B". They earn the same amount of income, and they both have one child. Family "A" does not have a high regard for education. The father is abusive to his wife and child thinking that physical punishment is the way to solve problems of disobedience to his authority. He has little time for his child since both he and his wife must work to support the family, and what time he does have he uses to amuse himself...TV, sports, beer, and occasionally drugs. He seldom reads or thinks about much other than his "toys" and how to acquire more of the same. The mother says that she loves her child but unfortunately has little time to express it since she has a full time job and no help from her husband with the household chores. She is usually tired or depressed and her husband's demands come first anyway. The family seldom eats together...meals are often catch as catch can. Rather than gathering around the kitchen table for meals as a family, it's usually at the TV set, which is always on to watch sitcoms, MTV, or sports...boxing, basketball, football, etc. Neither parent takes much interest in the child's schoolwork except to berate him should the school contact them over his behavior or lack thereof. The family construct is built mostly on lies...child lies about friends and activities, wife lies about her feelings, husband lies whenever he needs to. I could go on but you get the picture.

In contrast to family "A", although both parents also work, family "B" makes an effort to program what time they have to be together and listen to each other. Dinnertime is filled with discussion of the day's events. The parents react positively to one another and are keenly aware of their child's development. Father and mother have a deep interest in the community and the world. They participate at the child's school activities. Education plays an important role in family life. Their relationship is built on love, honesty, and trust. I could say more, but again, you get the picture.

Now, how do these children "see" themselves? This is crucial because, in reality, the way they see themselves is what forms their conscience. Child "A" has no trouble lying or cheating. It doesn't bother his conscience at all because that is what he expects of himself having been disbelieved so often by his parents as well as having observed their behavior toward one another. It all seems perfectly normal to him because that's the way he sees himself. That's the way he projects himself onto his friends and the rest of the world; after all, to him his behavior meets the expectation of a person who isn't any good. In short, that's the way he was raised, as if he were worthless.

On the other hand, child "B" has difficulty lying and cheating because that's not the way he was raised, and his conscience would bother him if he did because he sees himself as an honest, trustworthy person. Although he may wish to lie or cheat on some occasions, he will have to battle his conscience to do so. From these examples, it is easy to understand the role family and environment play in society. Although our early self-image may alter as we mature, it requires a change in the way we think and act to do so. Projecting this concept of self still further, how do we see ourselves as a family, a culture, a nation or a race? How do our myths compare with reality? Knowing the answers to these questions is the WHY that explains what we do.

There's one other observation I'd like to make. Many Christians would have us believe that God dictated *The Holy Bible* to man through revelations. But certainly, if God had written it, there wouldn't be so many inconsistencies; maybe instead of holy it should be called a "holey" book. There's no doubt, at least in my mind, that men wrote it rather than God, and like many things men do, they got a lot of it wrong.

Here's a thought! What if women had written the bible instead of men? It definitely would have been more consistent, and perhaps we might have learned that God created women first rather than the other way around. It could be that men are merely God's afterthought to amuse women, and furthermore, men would be in a much sorrier state than they are if women hadn't been made first in order to take care of them. Maybe not...it's just a theory of mine. Think about it, almost every sensitive bone in man's body is because of women. Without the distaff side, men would have remained savages, and killed themselves off long ago.

As I see it, God's only choice was to create

women first. The truth is that women instinctively care about life, and it's only by learning to care that mankind will survive. Mothers care. Look at the animal kingdom...mothers care so much about their young that they will sacrifice their own lives. Watch matriarchal elephants guarding the calves while they guide the herd to watering holes or mice carrying their young on their backs when rousted from a nest. All animals from the highest to the lowest instinctively care...it's built into the system, and they seemingly don't have the ability not to care since caring is so crucial to their survival. The reason caring appears stronger in the female than the male is because it's her task to nurture. After all, the male only drops the seed, while the female does most of the work. Is it any wonder she cares? On the other hand, unlike the animal kingdom, human beings have the freedom to care or not to care...you know...free will. Like most things in life, human beings have a choice that other animals don't have.

It seems as though women let men take most of the credit even if not deserved. In other words, women get joy by giving joy. It's well known that every great man can be traced to a great mom or mate. That's where men learn to love and care, and once love is experienced, there is no greater ecstasy. God knew that caring is a fabulous formula for happiness...after all, Mother Nature is

41

a prodigious creator. Conversely, not caring is surely the formula for pure disaster. Think about what happens when we don't care about ourselves...about each other...about nature. It could reasonably be argued that almost all of our problems stem in part from not caring. Can there still be any doubt that negativity destroys and positivism creates?

Life's bounty includes many benefits but one of the most common and rewarding is joy. There are many different kinds of joy, of course. Some of which are more admirable than others: the joy of revenge, the joy of winning, the joy of receiving a gift, the temporary joy derived from drugs to name a few. But there is a lasting inner "pure" joy that comes from giving of oneself, and we have all experienced it to some degree or other. Consider the joy a parent feels when their child succeeds or the joy felt from doing a selfless act to help a fellow human being. This is a different kind of joy and we all can recognize the difference. An example comes to mind of professional golfer Tiger Woods who gave millions of dollars to create a school for disadvantaged youths. In a television interview he said that it meant more to him than anything he had ever done. It was a joy that, according to him, surpassed all of his other accomplishments. It was the joy of selfless giving...pure lasting inner joy. These are benefits worth having and benefits that are attainable by each of us. Sadly, a number of years later Mr. Woods' frailty for women was exposed resulting in public humiliation and marital distress. It would be hard to calculate the devastation brought upon others and ourselves because of poor personal choices.

Some examples of nonphysical positive choice that define the best in human nature are: *love* rather than hate, *concern* rather than indifference, *compassion* rather than cruelty, *inclusion* rather than exclusion, *ethical* rather than amoral, *caring* rather than uncaring, *generosity* rather than selfishness, *forgiveness* rather than animosity, *understanding* rather than ignorance, *honesty* rather than dishonesty, *moderation* rather than excess, *justice* rather than injustice, *freedom* rather than enslavement, *humility* rather than boastfulness, *valor* rather than cowardice, *decency* rather than vulgarity.... These are only a few of the idealistic choices that reward us all and fulfill our potential. Acting on them discloses our humanity and brings a joy that radiates to others.

Over time our choices create an individual world for each of us, a world unto itself...orbiting through life with magnetic response to people, thoughts, and actions as we search for ways to demonstrate or sometimes to hide who we really are. In the process, we create a separate, different language born of our own experiences using the same words and actions that others use but with subtle and not so subtle differences that interfere with understanding one another. Transmitting my world to yours or yours to mine is an impossible task. Writers carefully hone words for readers that readers can never fully comprehend. We are each forever alone with no "great escape" from ourselves, and although we may reach out, we can never connect completely. Only we can truly know what is in our heart, and after all, that's the crux of the matter, isn't it? In the final analysis we are each responsible for what we think and do.

Apprehensively the question may arise, is there an afterlife to reward or punish us for our thoughts and behavior? For those concerned, it may or may not be comforting to realize that, as previously noted, eternal nonphysical abstract laws exist; therefore, conceivably other entities might also...a soul for instance. Whether it does or not is a matter of faith or speculation to be resolved at a later time for everyone. For now, however, Heaven and Hell are made here on earth as a result of our choices, moral conscience, and relationship to others.

With this regard, there's a lot that can be learned from an oak tree...majestic and strong yet at the same time very fragile...each one different in its own way. They produce thousands of acorns impregnated with life only requiring the right soil, water, and sunlight to fulfill their destiny, yet very few ever reach the potential of full maturity. The root system extends to the perimeter of the canopy and is so delicate that without the right environment rot and decay can develop to destroy the tree. Oak roots rival in importance the treetop and consume up to 300 gallons of water a day to support nature's miraculous system of photosynthesis. The root structure is the tree's foundation keeping it alive and preparing it for whatever contests the elements may bring.

Analogous to the unseen root system of the oak is for us a belief system of inner convictions. Our philosophy of life and how we think has a great deal to do with what we become; it is the essence of who we are and what we project to those around us. To this end, responsive successful individuals able to withstand the rigors of modern life rely on a philosophy based in truth and the sunlight of reality. Conversely, uncertain perceptions, a lack of ideals, or mimicry of deceptive, misleading ideas expose us to the contagion of moral decay and dysfunction.

Understanding proper relationships with one an-other and the world affects behavior, and guards against thinking that our beliefs are the only truths, the consequence of which relegates others to an inferior status promoting bigotry and condescension. Certainly, to act without self-knowledge is often regrettable. Yet sadly this journey to understanding our humanity may take a lifetime for some. Hence, a question of central importance becomes "What is our purpose in life?" The same question could be asked regarding other creatures; however, they seem to know what is expected of them. Only human beings find themselves in a quandary about their purpose in life, and it affects the way we live and the happiness we find. The best answer to the question of purpose that I can think of is: to experience the fullest, greatest potential of our humanity. Part of this endeavor requires the act of believing.

A hostile world can be a very scary place. It's little wonder then that mankind seeks refuge in a supreme being to assuage anxious fears and give hope to the future. It's also little wonder that religions have capitalized on this insecurity with mysterious revelations, dogma, and ritual. In consequence, solace is often derived by giving a deity heightened heroic, mystical powers. Undoubtedly, evolving concepts of God in various cultures and historical periods more than anything else reflect our fears and needs thereby distorting the reality of God...assuming that deities exist. In many ways mankind has projected onto Gods super-human versions of our own capacity: the potential of revenge, brutality, enigma, love, forgiveness, creativity, intelligence, etc., etc. Rather than assign these capabilities to God, "re-own it", as the self-help book *I'm OK, You're OK* suggests in regard to analyzing personal relationships. Often people project onto others their own failings as well as abilities without realizing it. By ascribing our intrinsic powers to God, we denude human capacity; therefore, acknowledge our capabilities. Much of "God" is the result of projections that we have made...take back those powers...re-own them. Believe in our human potential. Respect it, nurture it, use it.

While acknowledging the aforesaid, fundamental to life's purpose is our perception of God, assuming that there is a God, and the relationship between us. "Who cares? Let's just have fun! If it feels good, do it! What difference does it make?" some might say. But suppose we had a job and we didn't know who the employer was, what the company expected of us, what our relationship to other employees was, or what the benefits were. How successful would we be? Not very is the answer. Likewise, in life we need to know how the system works and our place in it to find personal gratification and not fall into negative patterns of behavior.

Who or what then is this moving force which some call God? Unfortunately, there doesn't seem to be a uniform answer or agreement on the concept of God. Yes, most people in the western world and the Near East would say that there is only one God and are monotheistic while millions of Asians are polytheistic, but whose God are we talking about since everyone seems to have their own somewhat vague idea on the subject anyway, and religions haven't helped or agreed on it since the beginning of time. As a consequence, God is often divisive. What we have is about as many Gods as there are people...except for the atheists, of course. Who can blame them for not believing when we have made the nature of God so befuddling and incomprehensible? What exactly is this God phenomenon that is thought by many to have created the universe, if it did in fact, and how do we find it, know it, define it, and benefit from it?

It's regrettable that we have given God the name "God" because the name carries with it the claptrap of centuries from visions of "hell-on-wheels" to "mister-nice-guy". Also, and regrettably for the concept of a deity, we human beings are very dependent on our sense of vision. In consequence, the word God conjures up various mental images, and no matter how hard we try not to visualize God, there is this looming, father-like, larger than life image that intrudes on our understanding of a deity. In fact, the masculine pronoun used with a capital "H" in reference to God says it all...God must be male...but why not a feminine pronoun? Does God have a gender? In point of fact, neither He, She, nor It is really an appropriate reference, and oddly enough, although God is seen as masculine, we refer to nature as Mother. Nevertheless, if women had had the leisure time to philosophize about a deity, the pronoun no doubt would be feminine. Alas, women were busy rearing children and looking after the needs of men; consequently, albeit an affront to women, God is masculine. A new personal pronoun is needed...one that isn't gender specific and helps us to think "outside the box" erasing visual images associated with personal pronouns. Though some may find the idea disconcerting, I am coining the word "IZ" for that purpose as a pronoun or synonym in reference to God. It isn't gender specific, and I use it interchangeably to help re-frame the God concept.

So, what is God? Well, it certainly isn't some kind of superhuman being or any kind of matter or substance up in the sky or anywhere else. It isn't even intelligence as we think of intelligence because intelligence requires a mind and a mind infers matter...neurons, synapses, cells, etc. Where would this "mind" be located anyway?

There is a hierarchy of intelligence in the universe that can be observed in various animal forms culminating with human beings and ultimately "God", assuming IZ exists. The human level of intelligence is capable of understanding the ultimate intelligence but incapable of being or becoming that higher intelligence since the highest level is not composed of matter. The ultimate level consists of intangible fundamental abstractions and immutable concepts, rather than matter.

As stated before, matter could not exist without the nonphysical laws of science that rule over it. These abstract principles or laws, if I may call them that, exist whether or not we are here to observe them. They existed before the "big bang" of creativity and affect everything in the universe, everything in our world, everything in our life. They permeate our very being whether we believe them or not. They exist beyond time and space. They are eternal. They constitute the plans and building blocks of the universe, and they are neither judgmental nor happenstance. They are eternal truth, which like a circle of time has no beginning and no end. Some truths are only momentary…true today but perhaps untrue or less true at a later time; they are not eternal.

ETERNAL TRUTH is what God is. Eternal truth is not an entity devised...it just IS and always has been and will be. The antithesis of God mankind conceives through ignorance and negativism that contradict nonphysical positive truth.

Consider the game of chess...a game of intellectual skill. The game isn't the chessboard or chessmen, though they are required. The game is an intangible set of rules without which and adherence to there can be no chess game. And what sense would it make if the rules were changed on a whim or to satisfy one of the players and punish the other? None. Similarly, the universe operates on truths, immutable laws, and abstractions some of which are known and many yet unknown that comprise the game of life for the human family. This creative system is the "God phenomenon". Not only do these laws make life possible, but also the unending search for additional laws excites and rewards. We constantly struggle to learn more and express these verities with scientific formulas, logic, or artistry, in the realms of science, philosophy, and the arts. Were the physical universe not here, these truths would still exist. Man can choose them for his benefit or ignore them at his loss and sometimes peril. Defy the law of gravity, for instance, and you'll quickly understand what I mean.

It's said that we are what we eat, and most people probably agree with that. Eat good food in the proper amounts, and it's reflected in a healthy body…makes sense. It's also true that we are what we do, and our actions reflect what we believe. Sadly, while we may claim good values, our actions personally, culturally, and nationally often indicate otherwise. After all, the United States does have the largest percentage of prison inmates per capita in the world. What does that say about puritanical values and practices in America?

Value systems usually are learned in the home or a place of worship, but today families are fragmented and religion seemingly has little relevance to what is actually happening in the world. Every day we see people of prominence and responsibility as well as corporate entities and governments failing to meet even the most rudimentary ethical standards with little or no consequence to anyone other than the public. It's small wonder that the rest of us often don't feel compelled to do what's right. Millions struggle for basic needs while others, with little concern for the less fortunate, are awash in creature comforts. Society is in disarray. When the most pressing concerns are consumption, money, and self-indulgence, our future is indeed bleak. Like a swarm of locusts consuming everything in its path, we are headed for self-destruction, unless we can find something to alter our course. Obviously, there are serious problems needing attention. As filmmaker Michael Moore put it, our "me-me-me" society needs to invert the "M" in me into a "W" resulting in a "We" approach to life. But to my mind, it's even more than that; only a revolutionary change in the way we view life can alter our course.

We know for a certainty from school that proven formulas don't lie, and although we might, formulas don't; formulas are true. Presently, scientists aspire to develop one grand formula to explain the entire physical universe. Obviously, it's not easy, it's not simple...it takes time. But when they do find it, I believe it will be magnificently beautiful in its simplicity...just like the theory of relativity. People such as Albert Einstein and others who strive for truth are putting us on God's doorstep with their discoveries, because that's part of what God is, simply a grand formula. It's a formula that works because it's true. Would we pray and kowtow to "A" squared plus "B" squared equals "C" squared? Of course not...unless we're some kind of math nut. What we do is we use it for our benefit. God's grand universal formula doesn't talk to us. It doesn't take sides. It doesn't punish non-believers. It's a magnificent formulation of eternal truths on which the universe operates, and it's personal because it affects each of us and we can depend on it as surely as the sun comes up tomorrow.

Darwinian theory suggests that life operates through natural selection. This is a generative process for survival involving environment and cellular mutations whereby those that cannot adapt are left by the wayside while the others survive and multiply. Simplistically, it works somewhat the way we create things: trial and error until something clicks and makes sense. The accepted and established is revised or destroyed inevitably with each new creation. Although this process in Darwin's time was thought by some to occur without the guidance of The Creator, it must be remembered how IZ was conceptualized at the time. By today's more enlightened view, the selective aspect of creativity can be seen as part of the God phenomenon. After all, nature's selections are not senselessly idiotic.

Mindless selectivity doesn't require time, intention, or functionality. With Darwin's theory as one of the cornerstones of knowledge, the universe turns on a selectively evolving creative framework. Yet, the world is so constituted that we can depend on the constancy of natural and scientific laws. Thus, scientists become the equivalent of modern day clergymen searching for God's truth. Isn't it ironic that Darwin, who briefly contemplated being a clergyman before becoming a naturalist, tangentially contributes to the understanding of God?

A lot of people who believe that God is omnipotent and omniscient have trouble believing in the truth of evolution. Let me prove this principle to those who have little faith in science but a lot of faith in *The Holy Bible* with a bit of dialogue between God and Moses on Mount Sinai. God speaks first.

> "Hello, Moses, so good to see you. I'm your God, Yahweh. I've been expecting you. What took you so long? Oh, never mind I know what happened. Listen Moses, mind if I call you Moe?"
> "No, God, call me anything you like. This is a huge surprise."
> "Please, get off your knees, Moe. You and I need to discuss a few problems I've noticed with that ragtag bunch of followers you've got."
> "*Oy vay*, Lord. I've been wanting to talk to you about it, too."
> "The way I see it you fellas need some rules to follow so as to keep you straight and keep you out of trouble...call them commandments...that way it sounds a little more scary. (Moe nods in

agreement) I must say, Moe, I was expecting you to come up with this stuff on your own, but since you haven't and I have a few days off maybe I can help out."

"*Oy*, God, we can use all the help we can get. Anything...anything."

"Now, Moe, stop jumping up and down. Why don't you sit on that rock over there? I don't want to give you more than you can handle so, let's see, you're going to be here for about 40 days and 40 nights, right?"

"Yes, Lord, I needed to get away for a while. They're driving me *meshugge* down there. That's why I came up here."

"No need to go into that. I know why you're here."

"Just tell me everything, everything. We know so little about what's going on. I've got a real good memory and then I got my tablet and chisel."

"Moe, it's not that simple There's lots I could tell you...you know that I've been called omniscient, of course, and omnipotent, too. So I suppose I could tell you everything and get it over with, but I've got certain principles that I established and you guys are just gonna have to go along with me on this...know what I mean? No, of course you don't."

"So I'll try, I'll try..."

"Well, let me put it to you this way. There's a lot of stuff you'll get to know later on...stuff like the earth and its relationship to the sun, where you came from and what makes you tick...stuff like that...I'm thinking eons here, so we'll just start with the basics and see if you can handle them. We'll see how things EVOLVE. You know, I like to make changes now and then to keep from getting bored. Usually things don't come out perfect the first time anyway...I mean, look at Adam, for example. Let me see, for now, you know how to make a fire and you finally perfected a wheel, right, Moe? (Moses nods) That's a big step in the right direction. It's just this silly principle of mine that keeps me from spilling all the beans, if that makes any sense to you." (The Lord chuckles to Himself)

"Whatever. You know best, Lord. You know best."

"I sure do, Moe. Perfection takes a lot of time."

"Can I make you a sacrifice Lord? I got a lamb or two."

"That won't be necessary, Moe, if I need a lamb I know where to get them. Look, this is what I'm going to do for you. I'm gonna give you 10 rules over the next 40 days...I'll give you one every four days. Maybe you could chisel them out on your tablet. That way you'll have time to think about each one and let it sink in. Know what I mean. Moe? I don't want to overload the system."

"Gee, Lord. That's great. I can't wait to tell my two wives. This is gonna make me one *grossa kanocker* when they hear I was talking directly to you, Lord. What's the first one of these...ah, ah...er commandments?"

Well, you get the point. Since God is supposedly omnipotent and omniscient why wouldn't he just make the final version of the universe from the beginning? Think of how much time and effort could have been saved. Who needs evolution?

Theologians will agree that God is first and foremost a creator. An important aspect of the God phenomenon is the CREATIVE SPIRIT, and no matter how paltry our creativeness may be by comparison, in some ways it mirrors God's power. To me, one of the great wonders of human creativity is the wide range of emotions it stimulates: to challenge, excite, exhilarate, frustrate, agonize, and gratify, for example. The creative process engenders benefits from positive choices; yet sadly, some deliberately choose negativity, which is the antithesis of creativity and frequently is devastating to all of us.

God is a formula for life...physical and otherwise. My Dad once said that it's like electricity. We can't see it, but we see the results and we know that it works. That's true, of course, unless we make a poor choice and connect the wrong wires. ZAP! We get a jolt. Wake up! We're messing with the electrical formula. Fortunately, the formula for man is extremely simple...simple so that we can each understand it without excuses: DO WHAT'S RIGHT! It is the essence of morality. To want for others what we would want for ourselves...universally that's really what "right" is, and it's an important precept for mankind. Sure, we have a potential of wrong choice, but prepare to get zapped because that's not the formula, and although sometimes doing what's right isn't as easy as it sounds, having the courage to pursue it strengthens and rewards us.

Yes, the formula for humankind is "do what's right". Basically, the God phenomenon is awesomely simple to understand...a formulated system on which the entire universe operates. If we don't follow the formulas, we get hurt and often hurt others in the process. It's not The Creator's fault. It's ours.

Now, if you're an atheist, please don't tell me that you don't believe in two plus two, but for those who may still doubt the existence of a creative force, let me ask this, "Can mathematics be removed from a numerical equation, can color be divorced from light, or can a creative intelligence be removed from a creation?" Even if we conclude that creation is random and has no particular meaning, a creative force is involved. Creativity equals an intelligence and purpose even when nonsensical. An inseparable relationship exists between intelligence and creation.

Examples of this creative connection abound. A rock, nature's mighty warehouse of mineral elements, begrudgingly succumbs to sledge or erosion; can anyone look deep inside to the atomic structure and say that intelligent creativity isn't present? A sunflower, standing tall and beautiful, synchronized with the sun...what is its purpose but to be the best sunflower it can be and produce seeds that will insure its immortality. Try to create "from scratch" even one of its cells and if you can, breathe life into it; then tell me that intelligence escapes the sunflower's creation...and what then of mankind or any part of the universe?

Surely, there are many unanswerable questions in the world. For instance, what is beyond infinity? What came before the beginning "bang"? Why is there a universe at all? What is its purpose? There aren't knowable answers to many questions. Often things are beyond our ken and some things apparently just "are". There will always be many puzzling conundrums which we may never solve, hard as we may try, but with respect to the phenomenon of God and experiences with our own creativity, I think we have to say that minimally creation requires an intelligence...so too with the universe, an intelligence beyond our full understanding, the awesomeness of God. Therefore, it isn't a question of IF there is a Creative Spirit. Call it what one will, a Creative Force. an Intelligence, The Almighty, IZ, Allah, Yahweh, or God, to deny its existence is as absurd as believing that man lived with dinosaurs millions of years ago. The question isn't does "God" exist? The question is: Is the "God" of any given religion construed in a rational manner so that we can believe, or is there a more reasonable way which doesn't require dogma or a questionable leap of faith?

There's no doubt that untold good as well as evil have been done in the name of The Almighty and religion throughout the ages. Religious ranks have been filled with the willing in hopes of salvation and sometimes the unwilling on pain of death. Muhammad gained many a convert by threatening death to the unbelievers, and centuries later Emperor Charlemagne used the same ploy to gain Christian converts. Often religions have supplanted the inspirational, caring simplicity of "holy" men with ritual and dogma self-righteously seeking domination and control over others. If the ones whose names they champion could see the use of their exemplary lives today, they would be sorely disappointed.

With regard to Christianity, "holy ghost" and "holy spirit" give rise to very eerie pictures, as do the quixotic ideas of many religions. So, forget the vision in your mind. It's nonsense. Forget the preconceived notions religions foster. Forget the rituals and the theatrical trappings that make it all seem mysterious and unfathomable. This thing is as simple as two plus two and is not intended to confuse us. What would be the purpose making IZ complex and unfathomable to the ordinary person? Is God's largess meant only for a selected few pious intellectuals or zealots?

Unfortunately, reference to "God the Father" also poses a problem. Show me a father who wants his children prostrate before him, praying, pleading for mercy, worshiping him, and who then doles out rewards to the chosen submissive ones, and I'll show you a bad father. Every good parent wants their children to be respectful and loving, yes, but not from fear or hope for reward. Beyond that, they want them to learn independence, exploring their own person and the world with freedom to think and experience life on their own terms. Punishment is a non-issue; love and understanding are the hallmark of good parenting.

The Biblical and Islamic God of Abraham is a tyrant, and according to Christian belief, everyone is born in sin at conception...no wonder IZ is quick to punish unless strictly obeyed. What an ambivalent image--IZ loves us but wouldn't hesitate to throw us into Hell. The sign of a loving father isn't "It's my way or the highway". These absurd ritualistic and legalistic demands of religion are relics of the past based on limited understanding of the world at that time but continue as traditions that only confuse issues and repel thinking people. It's time to question authority and adapt to new realities lest dogmatic zealots destroy the future. Unfortunately, we have become intellectually lazy letting others do our thinking for us.

Thomas Paine, who almost single-handed is responsible for our War of Independence from England, believed that God was best revealed in nature not in Scriptures and in his enlightened book *The Age of Reason* wrote:

> "I do not believe in the creed professed by the Jewish church, by the Roman church, by the Greek church, by the Turkish church, by the Protestant church, nor by any church that I know of. My own mind is my own church."

Take just a moment and imagine that there are no religions in the world. Let time stop. The world remains as it is but without any religious institutions or ideologies. Now, shift gears to imagine something infinitely greater than humankind...some deity or entity, as well as a plan to promote its understanding and belief. Would any reasonable person even suggest ideas that exist in established religions today? Dietary laws, clothing laws, hygienic laws, golden streets in the sky, eternal fiery pits, reincarnations, demons, angels and archangels, vestal virgins, eternal life, virgin births, resurrections, Holy Ghost, Holy Father, holy wars, holy animals, holy water, holy smoke, holy books, holy grail, holy of holies, incantations, confessionals, dispensations, prayer direction, prayer beads, prayer walls, prayer carpets, gender biases, dubious theatrical rituals, and a raft of other questionable relics from the past just to name a few. It sounds like the Dark Ages...and indeed it is.

What's needed is a belief that is in harmony with science and nature so that we can use our power of reasoning to function constructively in the world without being asked to rely on deceptive religious revelations. Deism is that belief. Deism is the opposite of Atheism. Deists believe in God...Atheists don't. But Deists, unlike proponents of established religions, strip away dogma, ritual, fantasy, mysticism, and just plain old NON-sense from the equation to form Deism. Nature is their Bible. In other words, rather than basing belief on revelations from God as interpreted by man, Deists base belief on reason...the observable. It's faith in reason. It's reason over irrationality. It's belief in God without the "mojo".

George Washington, John Adams, Thomas Jefferson, Thomas Paine, Ethan Allen, and Benjamin Franklin as well as a host of other patriots of the American revolution, though members of established churches in order to participate in society, considered themselves primarily Deists and as a result, championed the separation of church and state...though not necessarily God and state. Why? Because they were painfully aware of the deleterious effect that the union of "church and state" had had in Europe, and they wanted to avoid that partnership at all cost. As for religion, Thomas Paine wrote, "The only religion that has not been invented, and that has in it every evidence of divine originality, is pure and simple Deism."

Thomas Paine candidly and powerfully expressed his views toward religion in *The Age of Reason*. Furthermore, he did not believe *The Holy Bible* to be the word of God rather he thought, "THE WORD OF GOD IS THE CREATION WE BEHOLD; and it is in *this word,* that God speaketh universally to man."

Paine's book, which was written over 200 years ago, is as powerful today as it was then and should be required reading for any person serious about understanding the God phenomenon. Abraham Lincoln found the idea of abolishing slavery in the writings of Thomas Paine, which had been written fifty years earlier. Lincoln's admiration of Paine began at the age of twenty-five, and he considered him his teacher, though his contact was only through Paine's books. Lincoln's law partner, Herndon, said that Paine "became a part of Lincoln." Paine enunciated social security and old age pensions as well as other social innovations in his blueprint of a good society. However, he held a low opinion of most religions:

"Every national church or religion has established itself by pretending some special mission from God, communicated to certain individuals.... Each of those churches show certain books, which they call "revelation", or the word of God. The Jews say, that their word of God was given by God to Moses, face to face; the Christians say, that their word of God came by divine inspiration; and the Turks say, that their word of God (the Koran) was brought by an angel from Heaven. Each of those churches accuse the other of unbelief; and for my own part, I disbelieve them all."

In Christian charity for their fellow man, oh yeah, Christians vilified Paine the rest of his life merely because he didn't agree with their definition of God, and he died in poverty as a result.

Religion has become a huge global tax-free industry using anxiety and fear as its raw material and dogmatic manipulation as the end product. However, for the past two hundred or more years since *The Age of Enlightenment*, science and philosophy have been putting religions based on revelations between a rock and a hard place by exposing the myths on which they rely. Obvious examples of myth are Jesus rising from the dead, Mohamed riding off to heaven on a winged stallion, or the thirty-nine virgins promised to

Jihad time bombs...why not an even fifty virgins? Speaking of which, it really stretches credulity to the breaking point. With the population explosion in Islam, where do they find all those virgins? Certainly not around here. It would take a huge supply to meet the demand. However, let's grant them an inexhaustible supply; there is still the problem of the meeting place. I might be able to accept the "truthiness", thank you Stephen Colbert, of the fable...that is Allah rewards faithful followers, but I can't believe the fable itself, and believing it is one of the requirements to join the club. Or how about this: what would you think if an illiterate camel driver told you that he had just hopped a flying horse over night from Mecca to Jerusalem and back so he could chat with Jesus and a bunch of deceased prophets? I know in a nutshell what I'd think.

These same requirements of faith are required of all revelatory religions. It's an imposition on sensibility to expect belief in the particulars of the fable and also to believe in the fundamental truth the story is trying to convey. After all, reason is reason and cannot be manipulated back and forth to satisfy deception. Aesop never expected his readers to believe such nonsense...the whole point is the moral...not the fable. Deists don't believe the fable part...only the truthiness part, wherever it may be found.

Most religions have sacred writings. The Hindus have Arya Sathya Vedam, the Hebrews study the Old Testament, Christians claim the Old and the New Testament, Islam follows the Koran, and the book for capitalist secularism is the Internal Revenue 1040...all designed to keep us out of trouble. The problem is that without exception these books require a host of theologians and clergy as well as CPAs and tax attorneys to interpret them for us and few of these experts agree with one another. I don't dispute that, with the exception of the IRS forms, all these texts have much to offer and are an expression of man's effort to understand himself and the world he inhabits, but can't we simplify this? Deists have already done it...God has written all that need be said in Nature and man's words cannot match its beauty. Science understands life in a rational way that can be proven and doesn't rely wholly on interpretation or revelation. As for the need of scriptures, Deists can sum it up in one sentence...Do what is right!

What's wrong with a person having revelations; don't we all have them? Yes, we do. That's what this book is for me and hopefully for you, though its contents may or may not be true...how would you know? I suppose you would know because you have had similar thoughts or it seems to make sense. In other words, though it may not be true, it seems reasonable. That's where religious revelations have a problem, reasonableness. Rather than use the word revelation since we're discussing it in a religious context, I prefer to say "an awareness" for what I write with regard to IZ. However, just because one has awareness or a revelation, doesn't mean that it's true even though it may seem as if it is, and it certainly doesn't mean that God gave it to you. Why? Because I just don't think God would do that even if IZ could. Doesn't it show a special bias?

I remember once or twice, when I was little, playing with a bunch kids and there would be someone who had a secret but who would only share it with just one or two of us even though we begged for it to be told to everyone. Sometimes unbeknown to us the secret might even be false, but their pleasure was derived by teasing the rest of us or by using their "secret" as a ploy to extract information and perhaps get us to do something we didn't want to do. Remember those times and how frustrated it made you feel? Do you see the bias? One kid is special...one kid is more deserving, and because of that the rest of us disliked the secret giver for manipulating us. That's just one of the problems with religious revelations.

First, were God to act in this manner it personifies IZ, and second, this biased representation of God would be disliked for favoring one person over all the others. It just makes common sense that here are better ways to reveal information, and even an anthropomorphic omniscient God is no dummy. When we have awareness or revelations, biomechanics of the mind are at work, and depending upon our talent and our perseverance, information is revealed in a multitude of channels. We prove their truth by examination with reason...not dogma, and yes, fantasy can reveal truth, too, but because we are rational, we recognize the fantasy as well as the truth for what it is. Our mental processes have come to us from God through evolution and in that sense one might say it comes from IZ, but God doesn't reveal anything to some kind of teacher's pet...instead a special resolute person uncovers truth with reason. God's secrets make up the puzzle of nature and human nature, which are designed to challenge the best of us. That's the contest in which we're engaged. It means we're not to take our talents frivolously, we're not to compromise them with drugs and demeaning amusements, we're to respect and nurture them because they represent the only survival kit on board.

Worship of a "God" has been practiced before pagan times to the present seeking special favors or as atonement for our own bad behavior and to what avail? Man is as cruel, corrupt, and greedy as

71

he has ever been only with more tools at his disposal to achieve dubious ends. Obviously, we must be doing something wrong because worship doesn't seem to be working. Oh yes, I can certainly understand wanting worship from others. It pumps up the old ego and makes one feel very important, but why would a God need worship? Ask yourself, "Why would a God want worship, let alone need it?" Are we intended to be submissive pleading pawns or is God so insecure lacking confidence and self-esteem?

Worship may comfort by giving a sense of communion with IZ, but one must wonder if God is interested in our pleas. Certainly, God is more likely to respond to action rather than words and ritual. Rewards in life accrue for those able to fulfill their innate potential. Unforeseen obstacles may thwart that potential in a hostile universe, but the goal doesn't change...not for nature and not for us. If we want to show our respect, gratitude, and worthiness for the gift of life, there is a better way to do it than worship. Fulfill the promise of humanity bestowed upon us. Fulfill the potential given. That's what IZ expects...that's the formula. Act in ways that honor creation by being the best person possible. Show respect for nature and other people. If God is a "father", make him proud. IZ doesn't need our worship. Replace it with rewarding actions that contribute to the world's potential thereby making it a better place for everyone.

To paraphrase the words of John F. Kennedy, ask not what your God can do for you, ask what you can do for God. For thousands and thousands of years mankind has been seeking help from God...and not necessarily the old fashioned way by working for it but by asking for it...a *quid pro quo* of sorts. In the good old days of paganism and early Judaism the sacrificial lamb was slaughtered to please God, and only later, much to the relief of the sheepherders, were prayers devised as a replacement. Since one prayer for one lamb might be insufficient reimbursement, Jews prayed three times a day as a consolation and the Muslims hoping to one-up-man-ship their neighbors raised the ante to five times a day...after all you don't get something for nothing. We do things for you, like worship, and you do something for us, like whatever we pray for. What kind of a relationship is this...certainly not one of love or respect?

It's more like a bartering system, and with the invention of money, clerics came up with a financial plan of paying dispensations for our lapses that I'm sure pleased God and filled the temple coffers immensely. This made things more than even steven and if you missed a prayer, they accepted your credit card. Is that the kind of relationship a parent has with a child or a loved one? I hope not, and it isn't the kind of relationship that's conducive to trust because if one of us feels cheated in the deal, they're going to be really upset. On the other hand as Deists see it, all that God asks is for us to fulfill our responsibility, our potential...God has already done the hard part and we get paid seven-fold just by doing what's right. Now there's a real bargain.

Furthermore, it seems to me that praying to the God of Abraham is inconsistent with logic. If IZ, is all knowing...past, present, and future, and all-powerful, then to petition IZ for favors makes no sense because God knows the future before it happens. Whatever prayed for would already be set in place one way or the other. God would know the change to be made prior to making it and so to remake what is already made is redundantly senseless...why would IZ ever need to reconsider? If God knows what the future is, IZ doesn't have to alter it...altering it belies knowing it in the first place. By this logic, prayer to God is a waste of time, though I might petition a person since they have freedom of choice to change their mind. Yet even then IZ supposedly knows what their response will be. In consequence, plead as one might, God never needs to second guess or change position...so why bother praying? One can't have it both ways, either God is omniscient and knows all, or one has to limit God's power and IZ doesn't know all.

And what's more, preachers, monks, priests and nuns, pray all the time and still unfortunate things happen to them just as it may to those who don't pray. Moreover, it doesn't prevent some of them from doing very evil things. Personally, I hope, but I don't pray. I can't alter the immutable laws of nature, and by definition, nothing can do it for me. Facetiously, when it comes to prayer and faith, I think the Pope sets a bad example by riding around in a bulletproof fish bowl. If anyone should have faith in God, it is the Pope...why then wouldn't IZ protect him from harm? Perhaps the Pope has more faith in bulletproof glass than he does in his God, or does he rationalize that his God provided bulletproof glass so as not to test his faith? Either way, the Pope is taking no chances. Deism doesn't require these kinds of mental gyrations; Deism is simply faith in the laws of nature that affect everything, and everyone, regardless of the kind of person they are; therefore, it is beneficial for us to learn from and understand nature.

Let's use God's gift of imagination for a moment. Suppose that you and I are from outer space and decide to spend some time meandering through the galaxies to see what we can see with our super-duper telescopic x-ray eyes.   Hey, this could qualify for biblical.

"Wow, what a great eon this is. We haven't had an eon like this in a long time. Yo, watch out, don't step in that blackhole or you'll ruin your new shoes."

"Thanks, I wasn't looking where I was going. Gee, what's this? Look at that little sweetie-pie of a planet."

"I can see it. It's very beautiful. I mean really beautiful. I've never seen anything else like it, have you?   Hey, wait a mini-eon. Holy blackhole. Look at what's happening: all those little two legged creatures...I read somewhere they're called people...for some reason they're blowing themselves up...there must be millions and millions of them...ugh, blood all over the place...very messy."

"Holy Jupiter! That's not all. Look at the blackhole they're pouring into their atmosphere and their water...it's practically a sewer down there. What's wrong with them anyway."

"Geez, at this rate between blowing themselves up and putting all that toxic blackhole everywhere, I give them maybe one or two eons before they're toast. What d'ya think?"

"If that...maybe half an eon. And just what the blackhole are those people over there doing? They look like a bunch of bobble-heads. Look, that guy's putting a piece of paper in a crack and then banging his head against the wall. Crazy! Check out Intergalactic Google and find out what it means, would ya."

"It says here they're praying to a No-see-um they call god."

"Check it out. A whole bunch of guys down on their knees on some kind of little rug five times each time the planet spins...Hmmm, funny, I don't see any women. Oh, yeah, I see some now. They're in that building with the spikes...Holy comet, they're down on their knees, too, and burning little candles while that funny looking guy in front does something or other..."

"Wow, what a No-see-um this must be. Intergalactic Google says that it's supposed to know everything past, present, and future and they think it has power to change anything and everything. So they pray to it all the time hoping it'll change things."

"I thought prayer was some kind of pagan ritual. I guess they think it works.

It doesn't make any sense though, does it?"

"Yeah, I know what you mean. They're praying to change things now or some time in the future when they should really be praying to change the past."

"Right! If the No-see-um is so powerful and can change the future, why wouldn't it be able to change the past...then they wouldn't be in the mess they're in."

"I get your point. They must not be the brightest star in the sky, 'cuz they sure don't make much sense."

"Well, look my friend, this has been a very interesting eon for sure, but if I don't get home, my wife will kill me. We can talk about it later."

"Just give me a mini-eon and I'll be with you. Oops, I stepped in some blackhole. You better go on ahead and I'll catch ya in a couple of eons."

Now that I've had my fun, let me re-emphasize the absurdity of prayer to an Almighty IZ. Many selfishly seek a God that is a personal responder on beck and call...their servant to win ballgames, make money, and bring them luck, etc. Needless to say, that is not what God does...those things are up to us. Logically, if IZ has the power to alter the future, then IZ must also be able to alter the past. If God has limitless almighty power as some would claim, this is not beyond reach. Therefore, it is no more ridiculous to petition God about the past than it is about the future. Case closed.

God merely provides the "possibilities" for us to alter circumstances; it is up to us to make things happen with positive choices. The only way to change the present or the future is for man to act…hopefully in a positive approach, and the past will forever be, sorry to say, what we have made of it. Having said that, recent scientific studies indicate evidence showing the possible efficacy of prayer; however, I prefer not to use the word "prayer" in a religious context because most people believe that God somehow is responding to them personally. I prefer to think that the character of the natural world, created by God, has built into the system "force or energy fields" that respond when we integrate them with our thoughts…in that sense, God may answer our prayers, but when that happens, we are merely utilizing a structure of nature that IZ has already provided for our use. This does not mean that immutable nonphysical laws of nature conveniently will be altered for our gratification. Rather, it means that we have an innate ability to align our thoughts and feelings with nature in a positive way to ameliorate present and future conditions. One might think of it as an outwardly directed form of psycho-cybernetics...a natural phenomenon, one of God's tools.

Often resonating with the tenets of philosophy and established religions, nonphysical truths suggest that POSITIVE CHOICE gives balance and equilibrium to life. Acting on positive options elicits a rewarding, uplifting sense of satisfaction and elation. This is nature's response to positive choices. Therefore, the key to fulfillment is acting with intelligent creative choices rather than with the passivity of supplication to a God of the cosmos. Prayer of this nature may act as an emotional poultice to encourage choice and commitment, but God's gifts come as the result of our actions more than our prayers.

While our creativity emanates from nature and distinguishes us from other creatures, it waits to be utilized within each person. Creativity in all its positive forms is the fulfillment of our humanity as well as the solution to many of life's difficulties. Selectivity separates the ordinary from the ideal in the fine arts as well as the art of living: the right brush stroke, the precise word, the unforgettable musical phrase, the courage of conviction. Be loving, be generous, be peaceful, be fair.... It's all part of the formula. As a philosopher once wrote, "Life is NOT getting and having; it's BEING AND

BECOMING". Pay attention to the formulas, and don't believe the old saw, "the one at the end of life with the most toys wins".

The universe and creativity have been freely given to us all. Beyond that, we must earn rewards by using our imagination and intelligence. Although creativity is not necessarily a smooth or easy road, it is the path to personal fulfillment and realization of our greatest potential. When at times violence, tragedy, or misfortune fatefully strike, our response requires courage if we are to survive and recover. Positive choice can inspire hope and affect attitudes that promote success, whereas failure to heed nonphysical truths often results in catastrophe and pain. Literature is filled with the consequences of negative choice as well as heroic tales of larger than life characters destroyed by one "tragic flaw". Thoughtfully, we need to learn from such examples. Perhaps it would help if life came with a warning label to remind us that negative choices can be a dangerous trap.

Since life is often a difficult struggle, many may ask how can there be a loving God? Wouldn't a loving God make life easier? Not necessarily...the IZ formula is to challenge us, not spoil us. As parents we demonstrate love for our children by trying to give them all the resources at our disposal to succeed and then freedom to utilize or not utilize those resources while pursuing their dreams. Although we can encourage, we cannot live their lives or make their choices for them; we cannot fight their personal struggles, and if we try to, it's usually disastrous for everyone concerned. It is their life to achieve.

Likewise, God wants us to succeed and gives us the tools to make it possible: eternal abstract truths, freedom, intellectual curiosity, and creativity. What more wondrous loving gifts could be bestowed upon us? It is up to us to embrace them. It is up to us to accept our interdependency with compassionate concern for each other and for creation. When we do, life's struggle is assuaged and rewarded. Furthermore and importantly, God's eternal grace is forgiving. Poor choices can always be rectified to begin anew, but when we act inappropriately whether out of ignorance, pride, or selfishness, the struggle becomes more difficult, if not impossible.

In evolutionary life species are intended to reach their fullest potential using given talents, and rewards await those that do. No, IZ doesn't write books, win ball games, or stop catastrophes; we best meet these challenges with intelligence and selectivity. Choice becomes the basis of character and character is the ship that brings us safely through storms of adversity. Positive choice, appropriate action, and resolution of dilemma based upon just principles gives life gratification and purpose. Not only that, our creative endowment is infinite and stimulates a full range of emotions that displays our oneness with each other and with nature.

Selectivity is the basis of life in the tangible and the nonphysical world. This process is sometimes shortened through inspiration, but inspiration is the distillation of conscious and unconscious thought ultimately requiring analysis before choice. Creative selectivity is the formulary foundation of the universe, and it is our pathway to salvation in the here and now. Is this concept practical? Does it work? The answer is a definite yes, when we believe its truth and practice what we believe.

In the words of Thomas Paine, "Every religion is a good that teaches man to be good; and I know of none that instructs him to be bad." However, it becomes necessary to question the authenticity and foundation of religions that rely on revelation because any religion to be believed must be grounded in truth. With the exception of Deism, which without dogma or ritual can more accurately be called a philosophical belief, religions depend upon "revelations" which have been secretly given to selected individuals. It's necessary for all believers to have faith in the visions of these so-called prophets or apostles of God. Unfortunately, the revelations cannot be verified in any way since their recipients had been dead long before the scriptures were written. In almost all instances the authorship of the supposed revelation is doubtful and the character, that is to say the veracity of the author, unknown. Unsubstantiated testimony of religious prophets can only be considered hearsay and therefore not credible.

Furthermore, in the case of Christianity, inclusion of scripture in *The Holy Bible* is the result of a vote by men of whom we know nothing, including their intentions, motives, or character. To make matters worse, the testimony of these dubious authors, which occurred hundreds of years after the fact and were translated by numerous scribes numerous times before being selected by unknown voters, seldom agree with one another, though it is supposed to be the word of "God". Either God was a liar, had Alzheimer disease, was so enfeebled from creating the universe that he couldn't keep his facts straight, or the words of the prophets cannot be the words of God...take your pick. With the exception mentioned below, I will leave the litany of these Biblical inconsistencies to Thomas Paine, who enunciates them in *The Age of Reason* with prosecutorial precision.

Is it any wonder that faith is a requirement of

religions based on revelation? Many of their own followers find it necessary to interpret scripture so as to make it rational. For instance, in the New Testament the miracle of the loaves and the fishes performed by Jesus might be interpreted to show that Jesus believed one's physical needs should be addressed before one's spiritual needs...rising from the dead after his crucifixion can be interpreted as the word of God through Jesus being resurrected throughout the world. Interpretation in this manner brings reason to what seems unreasonable. But, as Thomas Paine points out one cannot interpret in any reasonable way loving one's enemies as you would love yourself, for loving them is to reward them for bad behavior:

> "The maxim *of doing as we would be done unto* does not include this strange doctrine of loving enemies; for no man expects to be loved himself for his crime or for his enmity.
> "Those who preach this doctrine of loving their enemies, are in general the greatest persecutors, and they act consistently by doing so; for the doctrine is hypocritical, and it is natural that hypocrisy should act the reverse of what it preaches."

And then there are those who believe Scriptures

must be taken literally...for them all the miracles happened as written word for word, fanciful or not...though I don't quite understand how Christians of this persuasion explain it when Jesus says in John 10:9: "I am the door".

In his best-selling book, *The End of Faith,* Sam Harris provides the following observation on religious faith:

> "Tell a devout Christian his wife is cheating on him, or that frozen yogurt can make a man invisible, and he is likely to require as much evidence as anybody else, and to be persuaded only to the extent that you give it. Tell him that the book he keeps by his bed was written by an invisible deity who will punish him with fire for eternity if he fails to accept its every incredible claim, and he seems to require no evidence whatsoever."

Deism doesn't have this problem. There are no scriptures, no dogma, no tithing, no clergy, and the only ritual is to act in harmony with nature.

Think of the number of men who have claimed to be prophets. How many times was the world supposed to come to an end? Oh, sure, today we call the Jim Jones' of the world crazies, but are those who literally believe the New Testament Book of Revelations and apply it to the present, instead of seeing it as a symbolic code that Jews under Rome's tyranny would have understood, any different? Jones, with devastating results, just put it in wrong time frame. I, for one, do not want to squander my faith on other people's fantasies. Nonetheless, I shall respect your right to believe in anything you like, whether it be voodoo or the tooth fairy, and I hope that you will respect my right to believe differently. I prefer to have faith in what is known and can be substantiated with my own eyes or logic, and that, to me, is Deism.

Judaism, Christianity, and Islam, sprang from Abraham's supposed covenant with God, and like Gods at that time of history, Yahweh was a tribal God...the God of Israel. Yahweh had chosen Jews to be his special people, "the chosen people of God". As offshoots of a tribal religion, elements of tribalism remain, resulting in the sense that God is prejudiced to one side or the other. Moderates of these religions seem to work together harmoniously, but the right-wing conservative literals are entrenched in their scriptures unable to cooperate with any who think differently. In this rigid mindset negotiations with people of a different persuasion become impossible. Consequently, the flames of dissension and turmoil are easily politicized, camouflaging the real reasons for conflict, which are usually money and power.

For example, the conflict between Israelis and the Palestinians is in actuality a contest over property rights. Both parties lay claim the land on which they live and with the help of religion use violence to stir the pot. Ironically, though they preach love, they practice hate. Religion raises emotional fervor and gets in the way of a solution. If the contest were over a piece of property between two Israelis or two Palestinians, in both instances they would let a court decide and accept the consequences whether they liked it or not, but when religion is inserted into the equation, the dispute becomes violent and never ending. Think of the number of wars that have used religion as a catalyst. Deism is not tribal; it is a belief based on universal natural laws...not the desires of one people over another. With this advantage, Deism cannot be exploited as an excuse for violence; therefore, the real reasons for wars are more easily exposed, making wars less likely.

One of the key components of Christianity that is so enticing and compelling to many is that God is a personal God...he cares about me...so much so that if I behave myself, I'll be handsomely rewarded in some manner. However, I think there is something wrong with this egocentric concept in that it depends upon my doing something in hope of a reward rather than doing it because it is right to do. Furthermore, if I don't do what this God wants, IZ threatens me with punishment. The Lord is the great puppeteer controlling everything. Whatever freedom I may have is reined in using promises of redemption and salvation. It is a scenario in which many rely too heavily on The Almighty and less upon themselves...ah yes, prayer to God is the answer and forgiveness for me, too. Other religions don't contain this kind of personal component.

Think about the relationship between a creator and a creation. We have all created something at one time or another, be it an offspring, a garden, or a bank account. Do we care about it...of course, and the degree to which we care depends on how much effort we put into creating it. Students who participate little in school don't care much about school, while those who involve themselves completely, care a lot. Thus, I think God cares, and in this way it is personal for us because we are part of creation. If God has to be considered a loving friend and confidant as Christians would like to believe, then think of God's love as being the gift of creation along with the tools given each of us to better ourselves and reach our potential. We are God's beneficiaries, ergo loved ones. Our mind is our church…uses it reverently.

Regardless of how nice it might be to have IZ as a buddy, I am of the existentialist view that we are alone, and furthermore, I don't believe that God has emotions; principles are in themselves emotionless, unless one considers our emotions as an extension of IZ. In other words, God is neutral, but we are not. In Deism eternal principles exist and we live within their framework always subject to their consequences, be they joyous or otherwise. We are free to act as we choose knowing full well that we are accountable for our action.

The Christian idea that we are born in sin is preposterous. In fact, recent studies point to just the opposite as Dr. Tomasello states in his book *Why We Cooperate*, "Children are altruistic by nature"…another religious theory bites the dust. Deists see mankind in a positive light. The quintessential definition of God's omnipresence by Empedocles 450 years before Christ says it best: "The nature of God is a circle, of which the center is everywhere and the circumference is nowhere." How profoundly beautiful! God is everywhere in *Nature* and no clergy are required for us to identify with IZ.

With science as the handmaiden of God, we have boundless freedom to explore our potential. An atheistic scientist is an oxymoron. Scientists who say they don't believe in God are denying the worth of their own endeavors because what they search for and the foundation of their work is what Deists believe God is...TRUTH. Thank you Mr. Scientist for providing us the scriptures. The *principles* of God are everywhere and therefore in us...yes, God's creative power is within each and every one of us waiting to be discovered.

The Age of Enlightenment unlocked the shackles of oppressive authoritarian religions that had held sway for over a thousand years with the result that freedom of thought and expression developed at a level never seen before. As a result, religious ideologies came under the attack of reason, questioning the foundations of faith. Deism and atheism both emerged and dared to confront established belief systems. The line between atheism and Deism, to some may seem very faintly drawn. Once mysticism, ritual, and religious canons are stripped away, God is laid bare and man's relationship to a deity changes. With this in mind, an argument could be made that atheists can be as moral and righteous as any member of society, so why not be an atheist? Do people need God in today's world?

I think it was the philosopher Kierkegaard who observed that if there weren't a God, man would have to invent one. Perhaps it is time for a reevaluation of the old model in order to expose the failure of revelation within a belief system. However as I see it, atheism isn't the answer. Atheism suffers from two basic problems. First, it tends to be selfishly egocentric, and second, atheism puts man at the top of the heap...potentially leading to arrogance and absence of purpose. If there is nothing, then life has little meaning except to grasp for happiness and pleasure regardless of the consequences...it doesn't matter or how we get what we want.

Especially in times of adversity, the negative nature of an atheistic philosophy has the potential of destructive patterns. After all, atheism planted the seed of totalitarianism in the twentieth century. Conversely, belief in something greater promotes growth aimed at a higher purpose and, provided that freedom of thought is respected, encourages fulfillment of one's inner potential and respect for others. Once we acknowledge the presence of Deistic principles, our job is to comprehend and apply nature's discoveries. An impartial God gives us the tools; we do the work.

And may I say with regard to the neutrality of God's spirit that God doesn't bless, damn, or forgive anything. "God bless America" or "God damn it" are meaningless phrases. They are meaningless because they are over used and because IZ doesn't do those kinds of things; we do. For politician's information, God doesn't bless America; we bless it...bless it by being faithful to God's principle of doing what is right, which is to say, respecting and caring about other human beings and nature. To keep repeating either of these phrases cheapens the word God. As for forgiveness, that is our responsibility also. When used, it is the resolution of a hurt that eases pain for all concerned.

Lastly, religious authoritarianism has brought unnecessary death and suffering to countless millions of people through extremist interpretation of scriptures and religious wars. It is also true that religion has been painted here with a broad brush that doesn't reveal the whole picture or the diversity of belief.

In spite of the ridicule I have heaped upon revelatory faiths, they have much in common with Deism that is beautiful and true, and their words also inspire countless people throughout the world to be better than they might otherwise be. Many admirable people live their faith and are an inspiration to others. Let's not forget that throughout history much of the greatest art, music, literature, and architecture have been expressions of those who sincerely believed in and were inspired by their God. I have no quibble with the faithful who truly believe in their religion, though dependent on fable it may be; my argument is with those who have no beliefs, use faith to manipulate others, or profess to believe but live an unnecessary lie that could be rectified with reason. I acknowledge God's existence, but my faith is in reason not fable…reason given to me by God for a purpose. If I am to honor God as well as myself, then I must respect God's gift; by so doing my faith becomes unassailable and I think that is God's intention.

People belong to organizations for many reasons, not the least of which is companionship, often without fully knowing or sometimes caring what the tenets are of the organization they join. When it comes to religions, there are a diverse number of ideologies to choose within each sect, from the most liberal to the most conservative, but minimally the bottom line is this: If you wish to be a Jew, you must believe that God spoke with Moses on Mt. Sinai dictating the ten commandments. If you wish to be a Christian, you must believe in the virgin birth, the Holy Spirit, and the physical resurrection of Christ into Heaven. If you wish to be a Muslim, you must believe that Allah dictated the Koran to Mohammad and at his death he physically flew into Heaven on a winged horse. If you wish to be a Deist, you only have to believe that God's existence is disclosed through nature.

The idea of God becomes more poignant perhaps with a mythological tale from ancient Greece. It seems that once upon a time Grecian Gods were very concerned about man and his desire to become godlike. Man's behavior was considered an imminent threat to deity's domain of exclusivity. If man could become godlike, it would certainly dilute the real Gods' power and influence. People such as kings and emperors, the very intelligent, and the very rich already thought themselves to be almost demigods. So this was a very serious situation. The real Gods, even Apollo, Poseidon, and Aphrodite, were in near panic for fear that man would discover their secret with all its inherent perks. In consequence, a brainstorming confab with all the Gods was convened on Mt. Olympus to deal with the situation and find a solution to the problem, but all suggestions to resolve the issue seemed inadequate to insure that the power of God remain hidden from mankind. In the sky, under the sea...no place appeared safe from man's prying inventiveness. After much consternation and despair over their failure to find a solution, one inspired God cried, "EUREKA"...or words to that effect. All the Gods turned with bated breath and anticipation. Then the inspired God said, "I have the perfect solution!

We'll put it in them; then they'll never find it." And so they agreed to hide this quality in man himself, where it has resided ever since.

Although there may be many reasons why we haven't always had success finding these qualities, if we choose to, we can discover that godlike power through creativity. Creativity has no bounds. It can be as seemingly insignificant as "making someone's day" with a warm smile or nurturing children toward adulthood, and it can be as profound as great works of art or scientific and philosophical discoveries, but regardless the level of creativity, it begins with thoughtful choices that ultimately reveal our humanity.

Deism is found in nature and I am part of nature; therefore, since each of us is unique I would expect my ideas to contain an individual twist or emphasis that is most suitable for myself...perhaps the stress on making positive creative choices is that contribution. And there you have it, dear reader-- my revelations and I hope the answer to a lot of whys. They were brought to me by a butterfly rather than an angel, and no, God didn't speak to me or knock on my door...that was the woodpecker at work outside my window. What I have written, what insights I may or may not have had are the result of using reason and creativity...tools of God for sure. Hopefully, you find it logical and it gives as much meaning to your life as it does to mine...if not, please take your own journey and think before you discard mine.

The Past and the Future

Understanding is inextricably linked to experience. A very poor person cannot truly understand what it is to be wealthy nor a wealthy person what it is to be mired in the depths of poverty because each individual has a different mindset, and to understand what the other feels requires living it. Love is an abstract word, a poem, or a song, meaningless until it becomes an experiential joy and then no words can define it.

Have you ever really known fear? I don't mean fear you'll miss your bus...I mean mind wrenching fear. If you have, perhaps you have a very small idea of what it must have been like to have lived thousands of years ago. How else can one ever imagine what it was like for primitive tribes clinging to life in a very dangerous world? The closest thing that I can think of is life in the death

99

camps of World War Two or as a refugee today with all your belongings on your back and little hope for tomorrow. Fear, terrifying numbing fear...one must experience it to understand what it does to mind and body. Fear of death, fear of disease and malnutrition, fear for family, unending fear...fear that never goes away.

Thousands of years ago how did people, who had the same feelings that you and I have, cope with constant fear? The simple answer is a structured belief and acceptance of authority. Rules of conduct were established to please gods, gods that had been revealed or thought up to protect the tribe...gods of their ancestors. Leaders gave authenticity to authority by claiming god told them what was required and if not obeyed that same god would punish the errant. They understood pain, suffering, and punishment...it was the story of their life, and they obeyed. Another sure winner was the inclusion of an afterlife that would guarantee either perpetual misery or eternal comfort. They obeyed out of fear and ignorance with the reassuring belief that their god would protect them and punish their enemies.

Fear is a brainwashing ploy used even today...scare the public and they will do what you want...the ultimate manipulator used by governments, corporations, the media, parents, religion, and the school yard bully or anyone who seeks to control your life. Through the millennia techniques were refined as authoritarian religions gathered riches and control until finally in the seventeenth century the pent up anguish suffered by the masses erupted from the intelligentsia in a movement that was to change the world.

Known as The Age of Enlightenment, it is considered to have started with the writings of Sir Francis Bacon in England at the close of the Thirty Years' War and to have culminated with the French Revolution in the eighteenth century. Also recognized as The Age of Reason, thinkers of the period began an unstoppable intellectual movement to question all authority from ethics, government, philosophy, and aesthetics, to religion; it spread to all corners of Europe, the Near East, and the Americas.

Ignited by progressive thinking, their efforts launched the modern age and changed the way we see ourselves. Voltaire led the charge against religious intolerance and argued that secular life should take precedence over religious authoritarianism noting that throughout history wars and suffering were perpetrated on mankind in the name of religion. French intellectuals led by Denis Diderot and Jean le Rond d'Alembert published the *Encyclopedia*, which was the collective work of over 100 French thinkers to secularize learning and free society from suppression of the church, which was still mired in attitudes of The Middle Ages. A primary focus of the period was to use intellect and reason to solve problems in a practical way for the betterment of mankind while dispelling prevalent erroneous systems of thought.

French thinkers of the period formed a movement known as the *philosophes* and it was they who coined the word Deism to distinguish it from religions founded on revelation and mysticism. They believed religion should be based on reason and that knowledge of the natural and human world should be free of religious bias.

Intellectuals around the world were very much aware of the Enlightenment movement and its influence was to be felt in American where framers of the Declaration of Independence, who were for the most part Deists rather then Christians, demanded the separation of church and state. Although The Age of Enlightenment curtailed the church's influence and power, the church did not taken it lying down and castigated those who refuted its doctrine. Today, with a wide variety of sects and ideologies and a less defensive posture, the church has tried to reach an accommodation with modern science and those whose convictions lie elsewhere. With little leadership or organization and suppression from the church hierarchy, Deism is barely known today and even the founding fathers have been painted as Christians, though of course they were not. However, effort is underway to change all of that. Websites and blogs have sprung up on the Internet to inform the public and give them a choice between a rational God and established church fare.

Literally millions of people believe in a force or spirit of some kind that is not compatible with the antiquated God of Abraham but is well matched to the tenets of Deism; they just need to know that Deism exists. Established religious groups have the overwhelming advantage of a paid clergy, social interaction, extensive literature, history, music, infrastructure and time to further their aims, just as earlier Roman and Egyptian religions had advantages prior to the recognition of Christianity and Islam. However, as the public becomes better informed, Deism will grow and present other outlets for those who want to believe in something beyond themselves. Deism offers to serious thinking people what they want: both recognition of God and intellectual honesty that others, who are often tired of apologizing for the inconsistencies of their belief, can't provide. Furthermore, most people recognize that intellectual integrity is an essential for personal contentment and gratification...Deism is that solution.

I'd hate to tell you the amount of sleep I've lost over this book. For some reason, it seems that whatever ideas I get they only come at night, usually around two or three in the morning, and then I have to mull them over a long time hoping that I can remember them when I get up...geez, come on God, I'm not a young guy. Please, check my time zone first before delivery. Well, perhaps this entry will be my last, and I can get some sleep. I'd like to write about the future of Deism, but first, I need to relate a personal awakening or two.

As mentioned earlier, I was frequently seasick in the merchant marine, but there is a huge difference between sailing aboard a steamship and sailing a sailboat. Basically, the sailboat, in rhythm with nature, glides over water while powerboats cut through the water, and that difference is huge when it comes to comfort. Ridiculous as it may seem for someone who often got sick at sea, I have had three sailboats and relish the memories of sailing with friends and family.

I remember once that I couldn't wait to go sailing by myself. The macho idea of being alone and single-handling the boat had great appeal...what could be more fun, I thought? When I did go, it was a beautiful day for sailing...clear skies, a warm temperature and moderate breeze...perfect for sailing, but after about an hour, I looked around and realized that this was no fun at all...what was I doing out there by myself? I wanted to go home...and that's just what I did, never to sail by myself again.

It struck me for the first time that the fun of sailing was not sailing itself but rather sharing the experience with someone, and it didn't matter whether the other person just sat there enjoying the outdoors or participated in sailing. It was the sharing that mattered, and now that I think of it, one seldom sees a boat on the water without seeing a group of people enjoying each other's companionship. Sailing alone in the world is no fun. In order to enjoy life, there is an indefinable something within us that needs to be shared.

My second observation relates to the fact that there is a great difference between giving a gift and sharing one. Giving can have the onus of an obligation, and therefore, it may be problematic; is it an appropriate gift, how will it be received, does the recipient merit a gift and so forth? Think of it this way, what is the difference in buying a meal for someone as opposed to sharing it with him or her? In either case the recipient gets to enjoy the meal, but in the latter, you get the additional enjoyment by sharing one another...it's the difference between a one-way street and a two-way street.

If you watch the television show "Extreme Makeover: Home Edition", which I have on occasion, the first thing that you become aware of is the extreme enjoyment that those who build the house have in doing it and the extreme fun you have seeing the joy they get from giving. The house and all its contents could just as easily have been bought and given to whomever it was intended, without all the fuss, but the "fuss" is the fun...it's the sharing of the experience that matters as much as the gift being given.

With the above comments in mind, I believe that Deism should tap into the gift of sharing. How does that happen? Obviously, benefactors are needed and an organization needs to be formed to implement whatever plans immerge. This is already happening in a limited way as ideas are being undertaken to promote Deism by individuals as well as by the World Union of Deists. I believe that eventually the Internet can become an international meeting hall for Deism by connecting like-minded people in communities, locally and around the world, to share with one another in building experiences that benefit both the giver and the receiver. A Deism network should be established explicitly for discussion of projects, contributions of money and time, educating, sharing of experiences, and encouraging anyone regardless of their belief to join in the joy of sharing. Deism cannot flourish by competitively pointing out perceived deficiencies of other faiths; rather it must demonstrate its awakening potential experientially by creatively sharing human energy to build a better society.

Acknowledgments

First of all, I would like to thank my friend Glady Schwarz, who when she read my first "spoof" of religion suggested that I get more serious about what I was writing. The result of which was later sent to Professor Robinson, and his unexpected encouragement is responsible for *Why?...B'Cuz*. To this day, I don't know why a professor of his stature would have bothered to read my paper...but he did. I have a theory that people at the top enjoy helping the rest of us attain our goals...this is my proof, my experience with this modest booklet. To Cal McCrystal, who wrote the Foreword with such intellect and wit, I cannot thank you enough. Mike Mott, who did the cover design, captured the spirit of my book better than I could ever have hoped. The amazing thing is that other than Glady, I have never met any of these people before and still haven't to this day. I'd also like to thank my long time friend Martin Ingerson for his insight and support. Finally, to my wife Gerry whose generosity and fullness of heart have changed my life.

About the Author

####

Retired since 1990, Mr. Goozee, his wife Gerry, and their labradoodle Becky live at the end of a rural dirt road on a secluded, bucolic ranch nestled in the northern California foothills of Mendocino County, where a babbling creek, huge oaks, pine, fir and madrone trees are their only neighbors. When not busy with chores, time is devoted to gardening, puttering in the shop, or painting in his studio *(goozeepaintings.weebly.com).* Added zest to country living comes from vacation travel or day trading on the stock market.

E-mail: *deismsite@wildblue.net*

##########

Proceeds from the sale of this book are donated to furthering the understanding of Deism around the world

www.ingramcontent.com/pod-product-compliance
Lightning Source LLC
Chambersburg PA
CBHW031323040426

42443CB00005B/203

The Holy Spirit often tells me to reduce the speed of my motorbike when I am going too fast, so that I will not get into an accident. Once, while I was riding my motorbike, one of my hands became very numb. That put me in grave danger, as I could not properly handle my bike with only one hand. The Spirit of God told me to pray in tongues. I obeyed, and the numbness left my hand. Praise the Lord!

One day, when I was worshipping in church, my legs went numb and I collapsed onto the floor. I said in my heart to the Spirit, "No matter what happens to me, whether I am paralyzed or in a wheelchair, I am not afraid, for you are with me." Immediately, the numbness left my legs and I could walk.

On another occasion, the Holy Spirit spoke to me. He said, "Hot Soup"; that was His way of telling me there was a problem. A few days later, I felt a pain in the upper part of my back. The Holy Spirit told me to pray, and I did. The pain went away. I suffer from this kind of back pain occasionally, and it is always a manifestation of spiritual battles happening around me. The pain is a signal from the Holy Spirit to pray and engage in spiritual warfare.

Another time, the Angel of the Lord was beside me and I heard a voice calling me to fast (the voice sounded like a lady's voice). I obeyed, even though it meant that I had to miss my breakfast. For one whole year, I skipped breakfast and fasted in the mornings. Before that, I used to take a late breakfast and I would feel very sick after eating the food. But, after that one year of fasting, when I resumed taking my breakfast, I found that I had been healed of my after-breakfast sickness. Nowadays, I can take my breakfast at any time and I feel well throughout the day. Praise our Holy God!

Without the Holy Spirit, I can do nothing. He often informs me about big spiritual battles ahead. He helps me pray so that I can be covered by His protection over me. The Holy Spirit teaches me and holds my hand so that I can walk safely. He sharpens my spiritual senses so that I can detect and avoid danger.

The greatest thing in life is to know Jesus Christ. Every day I give thanks in prayer to the LORD for His protection and healing, His grace and favor, His mercy and goodness, and His many blessings. I thank Him for the holy wisdom I have received from Him and for His constant presence in my life. I rejoice that I will dwell in the house of the LORD forever.

CHAPTER 2

Miracles of Financial Blessings and Provision from Our Holy God

*B*efore I became a Christian many years ago, I made a deal with God: I told Him that, if He would help me set up a successful business, I would accept Christ. I then proceeded to start a courier service, although I did not know anything about doing business. We soon got into difficulties. We did not even have a single client. Then I received an idea from God — to fax advertisements to potential clients, telling them about our business. Soon all four of our phones started ringing and we had more clients than we could handle. That was the end of poverty for us; we had received abundant financial blessings from our Heavenly Father.

The Holy Spirit knows everything that is going to happen in the future. We should always listen to Him. One day, the only delivery man we employed in our courier business didn't turn up for work. He called and gave excuses as to why he couldn't come that day. This put us in a tight spot, as there were urgent deliveries to be made. There and then, I decided to look for another deliveryman but my wife objected to it. The Holy Spirit told me to go ahead and fight for it. So I quickly went and got a new deliveryman—and thank God I did, because the old one played us out; he never came back to work. Imagine what would have happened if I had not listened to the Holy Spirit but to my wife instead? We would have been in hot soup with our clients if we hadn't delivered the parcels on time!

Another occasion when God blessed me financially was when I wanted to sell my box van. The Spirit of God directed me to a name card in the van. The card was turned face downwards and I could not see the name on it; yet I sensed that was the dealer I was meant to call. I called him and ended up selling the van to him at a very high price. Praise God!

The LORD is forever in my life. Suddenly I am free of burdens and worries; God by His supernatural power has set my spirit free. My children have all completed their studies and I am ready to retire from my business. God told me to pass the business to the next generation. At first I thought about my sons; but then the Holy Spirit prompted me to give room to my daughters. My retirement plan is to serve the Lord. I desire to plant churches and see the whole nation of Singapore worship our Holy God.

God has blessed me so much in my life, even before I came to know Him. My wife grew up in a village. She had some education and stayed home to take care of the children in their younger days. At the time, I had not come to know the Lord. I started my courier business without any money, education or experience. I had no knowledge of the trade, nor did I receive support from anyone. I wanted my business to succeed; I wanted a truck with my business name on it; I wanted all my children to make it to the university.

I got it all—a truck, a successful business, and all my three children are university graduates. I am indeed blessed. I asked, "Why?" The Spirit of God replied that, even before I knew Him, He was already looking after me. The LORD Almighty cares for the poor and weak (like I was); He wants to pour out His abundant grace and mercy, holy wisdom, and protection on them.

The Holy Spirit cares for me. True! I used to bring a 500ml water bottle to work, but the Holy Spirit told me to take a 1.5 liter bottle instead. I did as He instructed and found that indeed the bigger bottle served me better. The Spirit of God often tells me to take healthy food and to drink carrot juice and hot tea. He also reminds me to cut my hair whenever it gets too long. The Holy Spirit knows our every need. He knows what we will need in the present and in the future.

The whole world is asking, "Where is God?" In answer to this question, I want to testify that God is with you all the time. Whenever you face difficulties, He is there for you. Whenever you are in trouble, the Holy Spirit will show up to help you. He will manifest His "super" power in your life. He is invincible. Everything He does is done superbly, magnificently, wonderfully. This is the truth. This is what I have experienced in my life for many years now.

I am very appreciative of all the Holy Spirit has done for me, and amazed and awed by His faithfulness and goodness. Everything He has done for me is done "sharp"—that is, powerfully and perfectly. Everything He told me would happen has come to pass; His predictions of future events have been 100 percent accurate!

CHAPTER 3

God Puts a Song in My Heart Every Day: the Joys of Being His Close Friend

On 14 April 2014, I woke up at 3am with a song in my heart. It sounded like someone was worshipping in me. Then I heard the Spirit of God say, "The Holy Spirit is blessing you."

The Holy Spirit sings in me. Many times I hear worship songs in my heart, and each time it is a different song. Like this one:

"I am a friend of God,
I am a friend of God.
Holy God calls me friend."

Once, unknown to me, mosquitoes were breeding in a glass of water left unattended in my home. The Holy Spirit told me about the mosquito larvae in the glass, and I quickly got rid of the water. If He had not alerted me, the larvae could have grown into mosquitoes that might have spread dengue fever to people in my home and neighborhood.

On another occasion, I needed to hook something onto a wall in my home. I was about to knock a hole in the wall, so that I could put the hook in; but the Spirit of God showed me a small hole that was already there in the wall. It was just the right size for my hook too! Certainly, He knows everything, even down to the tiniest little hole in my home.

One day, while I was in a Christian bookshop, the Holy Spirit directed me to a calendar on display in the shop. The calendar had big, bold Chinese words on it and smaller words in English. The Holy Spirit kept on prompting me to read the small print on the calendar, which I discovered were bible verses written in English. This is what I read:

"Blessed are the poor in spirit,
　　For theirs is the kingdom of heaven.
Blessed are those who mourn,
　　For they shall be comforted.
Blessed are the meek,
　　For they shall inherit the earth.

Blessed are those who hunger and thirst for righteousness,

For they shall be filled.

Blessed are the merciful,

For they shall obtain mercy.

Blessed are the pure in heart,

For they shall see God.

Blessed are the peacemakers,

For they shall be called sons of God.

Blessed are those who are persecuted for righteousness' sake,

For theirs is the kingdom of heaven.

Matthew 5: 3-10 (NKJV)

I bought the calendar and brought it home with me. Since then, the Holy Spirit has spoken to me every day through these bible verses, and they have been a blessing to me in my walk of faith with the Lord.

The Lord has also spoken powerfully to me to abide in His presence and in His Word. As it says in the Bible, unless we abide in Him, we are nothing and we can do nothing by ourselves.

Abide in Me, and I in you. As the branch cannot bear fruit of itself, unless it abides in the vine, neither can you, unless you abide in Me.

I am the vine, you are the branches. He who abides in Me, and I in him, bears much fruit; for without Me you can do nothing. If anyone does not abide in Me, he is cast out as a branch and is withered; and they gather them and throw them into the fire, and they are burned.

If you abide in Me, and My words abide in you, you will ask what you desire, and it shall be done for you. By this My Father is glorified, that you bear much fruit; so you will be My disciples.

As the Father loved Me, I also have loved you; abide in My love. If you keep My commandments, you will abide in My love, just as I have kept My Father's commandments and abide in His love.

These things I have spoken to you, that My joy may remain in you, and that your joy may be full. If you abide in Me, and My words abide in you, you will ask what you desire, and it shall be done for you.

John 15:4-11 (NKJV)

Who will be with me to face the darkest valley of trouble (*Psalm 23:4*)? Nobody; only you, LORD. Thank you very much, Lord Almighty. Though I may not understand all the plans you have for me, I know that my life is in your hands; and through the eyes of faith, I can clearly see that you are good all the time. I am sorry to see the body of Christ split into so many different denominations today; but praise God that we all worship the same Holy God, Jesus.

Jesus, you are my shepherd, you are my Lord, and you are my Holy God. Nothing compares to your promises. I put my trust in you, you are my Savior and my healer. Lord, I offer my life to you as a living sacrifice. Lord, there is none like you. I sing for joy at the works of your hands.

I heard a preacher on the internet saying that blessings are already given to us. How true! I have already received many blessings from God. Everything I have is from our Holy God. I did not know anything to begin with, but I have received holy wisdom from God.

I visited a church and heard the preacher say, "Where do you want to go? Go to God when you face the prospect of walking through the valley of the shadow of death." Yes, indeed, the Spirit of God gives us rest and peace. I stand wholeheartedly for the LORD our Holy God.

CHAPTER 4

Win Spiritual Wars with Praise and Worship Songs

$\mathcal{T}$he Spirit of God leads me to talk heart-to-heart with my Heavenly Father. He leads me to win spiritual battles when I sing praise and worship songs. The whole day long, I have peace in my heart as God's Spirit worships together with me. I lift up my hands and my heart to honor and worship the LORD because our Holy God's words are true.

On one occasion, I was facing some challenges and took the day off from work to seek the Lord. I was at home in my bedroom the whole day, listening to the praise and worship songs being played on my CD. As I sang along, praising and worshiping the LORD, I could sense the holy presence of God in my home. The Spirit of God assured me that my family members would be protected by Him.

The Holy Spirit revealed to me that there was "war + war" going on—meaning that there were waves after waves of spiritual warfare, with new wars added to the old ones, and with wars happening both in the spiritual realm and natural realm. However, the Holy Spirit assured me that He would handle this "war + war" and lead me into battle. The Holy Spirit would plan a path for my future. He assured me that God had a plan for my life, and He would turn things around for me. I knew that what the Holy Spirit had empowered would happen and what He had promised would come true.

I began listening to sermons on the internet, to strengthen myself spiritually and to prepare for the "war + war" that the Holy Spirit had told me about. I received holy wisdom from our Holy God. The Holy Spirit was doing all the planning for this spiritual warfare and I knew He would handle everything for me. The Holy Spirit is super-powerful and invincible.

For many years, my master bedroom was dim at night, even with the light on. This was because the only light in there was from a low-wattage bulb. Then, on the very first day when the "war + war" spiritual warfare began, the bulb blew. The Spirit of God, by His supernatural power, destroyed the bulb before my very eyes. I heard a crackling sound and the light went out—just like that! So, I was forced to change the bulb and, this time round, I installed a much brighter light.

The Spirit of God had to destroy the low-wattage bulb because, otherwise, I would not have changed it to a brighter light—and I needed the brighter light to be able to read the song sheets so that I could sing along with the worship songs on the CD. This would help prepare me for spiritual warfare.

One night, the Spirit of God said to me, "Fear no evil"; these words were meant to prepare me to face an impending danger. As midnight approached, my body began shaking as I sensed an evil presence in the room. I kept shouting out "fear no evil" many times, until the evil spirit was gone and my body had stopped shaking.

On another night, I saw a light strike down like lightning from heaven onto a wall of my home. It was the Holy Spirit releasing His divine power into my situation at the time. He spoke to me, telling me to receive power from God, and I knew that surely our Holy God would empower me. As it says in the Bible:

> "But you shall receive power when the Holy Spirit
> has come upon you; and you shall be witnesses to
> Me in Jerusalem, and in all Judea and Samaria, and
> to the end of the earth."
>
> *Acts 1:8 (NKJV)*

I know I belong to you, O Holy God! I know your Spirit sets me free. I do not fight alone but together with the Holy Spirit. The Holy Spirit is in command of my life and makes the best decisions for me. Those who were against me, I have forgotten all about them; but the Holy Spirit takes action on my behalf; the Holy Spirit is my Avenger.

At times, several people would come to me and point to me and start making negative remarks about me. But they soon shut up because God tightens His hold on them to stop them from talking or acting against me. Somehow, they can't think of what to say next (as we say in Singapore, they become "blur"), and so I end up being the one doing all the talking!

Blessed be the name of the LORD. His supernatural power saves, heals and protects us. His supernatural power is at work to deliver us from seemingly hopeless situations and to walk with us through the valley of the shadow of death. His supernatural power sharpens our ears to hear and to understand. His supernatural power gives us grace and rest.

CHAPTER 5

God Speaks to Me in Supernatural Ways

*F*or many years, I listened to Chinese worship songs on a CD—especially one song (我心旋律 or "Melody of My Heart" in English), which touched me deeply. Solemn tears would well up in my eyes, I would cry out, and my whole body would shake as I listened to this song. It was only much later that I realized the lyrics of the song were taken from *Psalm 23* in the Bible. It was just so miraculous and amazing, because the words of the Psalm and the lyrics of the song reflected so truly and accurately the story of my life.

I had a large poster made, with this Psalm on it and with the heading, *The Lord the Shepherd of His People*. This heading, too, was given to me by the Spirit of God. (A picture of the poster is shown on page 4 of this book.)

This poster, which I have displayed prominently in my living room, holds a special significance for me. One day I was at home in my living room, feeling scared because of the spiritual warfare going on in my life. As I fearfully lifted my hand to touch my face, the Spirit of God turned my head to face the poster. All of a sudden, I saw words floating out of the poster in a supernatural way—the words "fear no evil" (*Psalm 23:4*) were floating on the surface of the poster! I knew it was the Lord speaking to me and assuring me that I need not be afraid because He is my Shepherd and He will always keep me safe.

The Spirit of God has also used the poster to communicate with me on many other occasions. For example, He has commanded me to add the words "The Lord the Shepherd of His People" (from the poster heading) and "His name's sake" (from *Psalm 23:3*) to my testimony; that is, this book is written for His name's sake, to glorify the name of our Lord, the Shepherd of His people.

Surrounding the words of *Psalm 23* on this poster are images of angels engaged in spiritual warfare with supernatural power: there are angels praying and releasing their power; angels blowing trumpets in heaven and on earth; angels blowing flutes; angels opening their wings for prayer; and angels opening their wings to fight the enemy.

These images are not merely pictures; God has opened my spiritual eyes many times to see that there are really such angels in the spirit realm.

The Spirit of God placed my finger in my ear; this meant that He wanted me to continue listening to worship songs as I was writing this book. I was listening to the CD as it played the song, "God Will Make a Way"—how apt! I continued to listen to the rest of the songs; the whole CD was full of worship songs! Thank you very much, Spirit of God, for leading me to this marvelous CD that contained such inspiring songs:

> We give You glory, we give you honor,
> We give You everything we are;
> Lifting our hearts and hands before You...
> *From "We Give You Glory" by Don Moen*

Once when I was in bed, the Holy Spirit made my body itch all over so that I could not get to sleep. So I got up and began looking online for sermons. I chanced upon a pastor preaching about praying in tongues—exactly what I wanted to know about at the time! The Spirit of God said that this sermon was for me, and He moved my hand to dig my ear (which meant that He wanted me to listen attentively to the sermon). He said to me, "Holy Spirit"; meaning that this sermon was from the Holy Spirit. Anyone who wants to know about the goodness of praying in tongues should listen to this sermon; simply click on this video link: http://tiny.cc/trinity sermon 22jun14.

Whenever I switch on my computer to listen to preachers on the internet, God would lead me to the sermons or testimonies He wants me to watch. He would also guide me to take down notes all the way throughout the sermon. The Spirit of God would also instruct me as to what kind of sermon it is, and He would categorize the sermons into their respective ministries. And whenever a preacher preaches powerfully and seriously abides in God's Word, the Holy Spirit would tell me that that particular preacher has the Holy Spirit in him and "no running dog"—meaning that he is no sycophant and has no hidden agenda, but is someone who speaks the truth.

The Spirit of God doesn't like "running dogs". Many times, He would point to a "No Dogs Allowed" sign He was showing me. What He meant was that He wanted me to "get rid of the running dogs"—that is, the evil men who were influencing me at that point in my life. It was part of the preparation for spiritual warfare at the time. God's Spirit continued to call out to me, "Get rid of the running dogs." The Spirit of God said, "This is Holy God's rice bowl"—meaning, this matter is very important to God. So I obeyed.

The Spirit of God kept on teaching me from God's Word. When He first started talking to me about the Scriptures,

I couldn't understand much of what He said. But He still continued to talk to me and teach me.

The Holy Spirit acts in His supernatural power to get my mind to dwell often on the Bible. By His power, I keep chewing on God's Word—just like the animals chewing the cud (*Deuteronomy 14:6*). As it says in the Bible:

> Let the word of Christ dwell in you richly in all wisdom, teaching and admonishing one another in psalms and hymns and spiritual songs, singing with grace in your hearts to the Lord.
>
> *Colossians 3:16 (NKJV)*

Without the Holy Spirit, I would not be able to do anything. But He enables me to do everything that He calls me to do. As it says in the Bible:

> I can do all things through Christ who strengthens me.
>
> *Philippians 4:13 (NKJV)*

CHAPTER 6

God Cares for Me through All the Seasons of My Life

There was a period in my life when the Holy Spirit was not present. I had no urge to lift my hands or my heart in worship. I looked around at the congregation and wondered why they were not on fire for God. I had no patience to stay long in that church. After leaving, I began visiting other churches. But I was worried and desperate as I could not fit in. Then I attended a service at a charismatic church and, when I went back home, God told me, "This is your church." I joined this church and liked it.

One day I went to the coffee shop to get my morning cup of coffee but, before I could enjoy it, I heard God saying, "Fast!" Immediately, I obeyed Him and threw away the coffee. Then I began to fear that I would weaken and fall sick because I had missed my breakfast; but there was no need to fear because I continued to enjoy good health from God. In fact, the Holy Spirit goes everywhere with me and strengthens me in my work.

The Spirit of God makes me lie down in green pastures. The Spirit of God leads me beside still waters. Once, when I was worshipping in church, I found that I could not sing anymore because I had sung until my mouth was dry. But the Holy Spirit came to my help—suddenly I found my mouth wet again with saliva (express delivery by the supernatural power of the Holy Spirit!) and I could continue singing! Certainly, the Holy Spirit wanted me to continue praising and worshipping God!

God cares for me, even to the smallest details in my life. I used to suffer from back pain and God healed me; but every now and then I would get a relapse and once, while I was bathing, I asked God "Why?" The Spirit of God told me that it was to stop me from carrying heavy weights that would further injure my back. Sometimes, too, when I had a backache and did not apply a *Salonpas* pain-relieving patch to my back, God's Spirit would move my hand to scratch my back to tell me to put it on.

I wanted to make plans to contribute some money to the support of my mother; but the Holy Spirit told me to hold on first. I did not know why at the time. A few months later, she went home to be with the Lord. The Holy Spirit knew in advance what was going to happen to my mother, and that there was no need for me to make those arrangements for her support.

One morning, as I was getting ready for work, I heard God's voice saying, "Alone, alone, alone." At the time, I did not know why He said that. It took me more than ten years to find out why. I now understand that it was because He did not want me to associate with the evil people who were around me at the time.

The LORD is good all the time. Everything that has happened to me in my life was planned by God, although I may not understand why. I asked Him why it seemed as if I was living under a curse (because I often felt alone in life). The Holy Spirit replied that He had a purpose for everything that had happened in my life. I understood and highly praised the LORD!

Thank you, LORD. Glory to the LORD. I give all to you, LORD. My life is in you, LORD. Holy is the LORD. I will bless your name; I just want to thank you, LORD.

CHAPTER 7

A Message from the Spirit of God to All Christians

*D*ear Christians, please love the Spirit of God first, and then His power — not the other way around. Your love will touch Him to tears. Thank you very much.

The Holy Spirit said to me that those who are "sharp" (that is, those who are sensitive to His presence and leading; those who seek after deeper knowledge and understanding of Him), and who acknowledge Him, touch God's Spirit to tears. The Spirit of God is happy when people honor Him with the praise that is due to Him.

When I am in the presence of the Holy Spirit, I am moved to tears. The Spirit of God opens my eyes to see things unseen by human eyes: angels coming down from heaven, and spiritual beings in the earth's atmosphere. I have seen all these through the supernatural power of the Holy Spirit. Dear reader, you too can experience the power of God's Spirit in your life—very dynamic supernatural power! There are no words to describe it. Just have simple faith and believe that all things are possible with God. Just listen to the Holy Spirit. His words are true.

You must obey the Holy Spirit. In the beginning, as you live your life in this new way, in tune with the Holy Spirit, you might find it strange and different from your old way of life. But please press on; continue to live this new life in the Spirit, and everything will work out fine in the long run. You will be surprised at how you start to look at the world from a different perspective.

You will begin to see with new spiritual eyes, and God will reveal His secrets to you. Keep your mind on the things of God. Chew and meditate on His Word. You will like it very much. It is very precious. Persevere and the Holy Spirit will help you, for the battle belongs to the LORD.

"So do not fear, for I am with you;
    do not be dismayed, for I am your God.
I will strengthen you and help you;
I will uphold you with my
righteous right hand."

Isaiah 41:10

Jesus said, "I am the Way and the Truth and the Life." (*John 14:6, AMP*) I can testify that this is really true. I have witnessed His acts of supernatural power that you can't find anywhere else on Earth. Truly I tell you, dear reader, that our Holy God is real and living, and He is God of heaven and earth. At the beginning of my Christian life, I wanted to know more about God. I received healing, protection, holy wisdom, grace, and many blessings and miracles from God. I felt the close presence of Almighty God. All this happened in real life—my life!

God is faithful and He will supply all your needs. Dear Christian reader, I have good news for you: the Spirit of God is in you, and He wants to open Himself up to you and talk with you, just as He has with me. I have received powerful revelations from the Holy Spirit. My spirit is open to the Holy Spirit and we communicate with each other. The Spirit of God has shown me many things, clearly and powerfully; there is no limit to the wonders He continues to reveal to me, all in His own timing.

The Holy Spirit has cared for me ever since I accepted the Lord as my Savior. I wanted to know how I could serve Him, and He revealed to me new spiritual insights and opened my eyes to see things unseen by physical eyes. He led me to record the testimonies within these pages; in fact, this book came about as a result of my face-to-face encounters with the Holy Spirit. He commanded me to write it. He called it His "rice cooker" (that was His way of telling me that it was important to Him).

Brothers and Sisters, please help to tell people around the world about this book. If you have been touched or blessed by what is written in these pages, please share it with others, for His name's sake and for the purpose of bringing people to the Lord. From beginning to end, this book contains an important message from the Holy Spirit to the world.

The whole world needs the Holy Spirit. Within these pages are true eye-witness accounts and real-life proofs of how, when we open ourselves fully to God, the Spirit of God will be lively and active in our lives. We will see many miracles happening. Let us shine for Jesus. Let us make a difference in this world for the sake of our LORD. Thank you, dear reader.

> Then Jesus... said, "All authority in heaven and on earth has been given to me. Therefore go and make disciples of all nations, baptizing them in the name of the Father and of the Son and of the Holy Spirit, and teaching them to obey everything I have commanded you. And surely I am with you always, to the very end of the age."
>
> *Matthew 28: 18-20 (NIV)*

The Spirit of God gave me a vision of God disappearing into the water, causing waves to ripple and spread out. The spreading out of the waves represents the Gospel being shared freely and openly throughout the world.

> Love the LORD your God with all your heart, with all your soul, and with all your might.
>
> *Deuteronomy 6:5 (NKJV)*

Love the LORD your God with all your heart and with all your soul and with all your mind and with all your strength. You must get rid of whatever idols are in your life, for how else can you draw close to God? How can God have any harmony with an idol? No way, for He is a Holy God. As it says in the Bible:

> How can light live with darkness? And what harmony can there be between Christ and the devil? How can a Christian be a partner with one who doesn't believe? And what union can there be between God's temple and idols?
>
> For you are God's temple, the home of the living God, and God has said of you, "I will live in them and walk among them, and I will be their God and they shall be my people."
>
> *2 Corinthians 6: 14-16 (TLB)*

Everything I do is for our Holy God, to our Holy God, with our Holy God, from our Holy God, and through our Holy God. Whatever I do, doing it with God makes all the difference.

> Therefore, whether you eat or drink, or whatever you do, do all to the glory of God.
>
> *1 Corinthians 10:31 (NKJV)*

People tell me that I am a "nobody"; but I have the Spirit of God in my heart, and no one is greater than our Holy God. So, in God I am somebody, and I will continue to write testimonies that glorify God and bring His message of love and salvation to the whole world. As it says in the Bible:

> "I know your deeds. See, I have placed before you an open door that no one can shut. I know that you have little strength, yet you have kept my word and have not denied my name."
>
> *Revelation 3:8 (NIV)*

Thank you, Lord, for all your blessings. God directs my path and my life journey. He leads me to fulfill His plans for me and to do His will here on earth, by sharing my testimony around the world so that the whole world will praise the Lord.

God's promises in the Bible have come to pass in my life; everything in the Bible is true. I cherish the precious words of God and His holy presence in my life. As it says in the Book of Isaiah:

> For I am God—I only—and there is no other like
> me who can tell you what is going to happen. All
> I say will come to pass, for I do whatever I wish.
>
> *Isaiah 46: 9-10 (TLB)*

The Holy Spirit strengthens me and releases His supreme power to enable me to accomplish God's purposes for me. As it says in His Word:

> But those who wait on the Lord
> Shall renew their strength;
> They shall mount up with wings like eagles,
> They shall run and not be weary,
> They shall walk and not faint.
>
> *Isaiah 40:31 (NKJV)*

The Holy Spirit has called me to open my "wings" for spiritual battles and to fight to defend the Gospel. He has called me to open my "wings" for prayer. He has called me to open my "wings" to "shoot" with tears alone (meaning: to speak out strongly and boldly) with angels helping me, and for the cause of justice; and the Holy Spirit has said that, when I do so, God will promote me and I will arise.

> Arise, my people! Let your light shine for all the nations to see! For the glory of the Lord is streaming from you.
>
> *Isaiah 60:1 (TLB)*

I heard, out of the air, and received from our Holy God, the word, "begging". I felt very sad, as the tears of the LORD came into my eyes. My heart is begging to see the nations worship you, LORD! My heart is begging to serve you more. My heart is begging to know you more, for the sake of your people. My heart is begging to write more for you. My heart is begging that, in the darkness, we can see the Light.

My heart is begging and hoping that you, dear reader, will receive blessings, anointing and knowledge from God; that you will be touched by Him and be sensitive to His holy words; that God will set you on fire for Him, and that you will rise up for Him and start sharing the Gospel "sharp" (that is, in every excellent way) with people around you. As Jesus said in His Word:

> "If you cling to your life, you will lose it; but if you give it up for me, you will save it."
>
> *Matthew 10:39 (TLB)*

CHAPTER 8

God's Heartbeat:
His Call to Plant a Church

God cares deeply about what is happening in the world today. I had stopped listening to the news on the radio; but the Spirit of God commanded me to resume listening, so that I would know what was going on in the world.

Then, one night, as I lay on my bed, God supernaturally turned my head around (one big round, and I didn't do it of my own volition) so that I could see how the electrical wiring track went all the way up to the ceiling in my bedroom. That was a bit scary.

Then I heard God's Spirit speaking to me: "All the tracks go into the cupboard—long and short, all to hang in there." He had shown me the wiring track first, because that was His way of bringing to my mind the MRT (Mass

Rapid Transit) tracks, which at that time were often broken down. He meant that the broken tracks represented the life journeys of people with broken lives. People from all walks of life—whether "long" or "short" types—had their lives hanging in disorder, much like the broken-down tracks.

I have always wanted to plant a church, to reach out to the unsaved people with broken lives. At an early stage of my Christian walk, when I first received my salvation, my church leader (at the time) asked me, "How do you want to serve the Lord?"

I replied, "I want to plant a church."

My leader said, "Tell me that in the future."

Ten years later, I received a call (through a vision) from our Holy God to plant a church. But because I felt inadequate, I rejected the vision. My excuses were that I was "unable" because I was "too old" by then, and besides I saw no way to accomplish the task.

However, the vision appeared again, calling me to plant a church. The Spirit of God assured me that He would make a way. I received holy wisdom from our Holy God to start a ministry for tourists and foreigners coming from all over the world to Singapore. The Holy Spirit encourages visitors to my church to worship the LORD daily during office hours.

I received another vision from the Spirit of God: that those in darkness would see the Light—that is, they would see God. As it says in the Bible:

> "[O]pen their eyes, in order to turn them **from darkness to light**, and from the power of Satan to God, that they may receive forgiveness of sins and an inheritance among those who are sanctified by faith in Me."
>
> *Acts 26:18 (NKJV)*

In my vision, I saw lighted candles. I received our Holy God's command, that it was His will for me to have lighted-up candles in the church I was to plant, which would be called the Spirit of God Christian Church. I welcome everyone to worship the LORD daily during office hours at this church. My purpose is to lead people to Christ.

Nothing is impossible for the LORD. As I obeyed His command to offer my tithes to the church, I was amazed at the many miracles I was receiving from Him. I also received holy wisdom from God to use the tithes to print this book and to utilize the profits from the sales of the book to plant the church. I received revelations from God, too, that it was His plan for the church to start a ministry for tourists and foreign workers; and to call from among them certain people who could serve in the church as helpers.

The church is the greatest holy place of worship. When I was called to plant the Spirit of God Christian Church, I received specific instructions from our Holy God regarding the physical arrangements and design of the church. As I mentioned earlier, I had received a vision of candles in the church; so, in obedience to God's will and command, there will be candles lighted up during church services. I will also be installing a marble cross that holds a special significance for me. I will talk more about this cross later, in Chapter 10 of this book.

I intend this to be a church that will bow down in unison to pray to the Lord. As it says in the Bible, "God is spirit, and his worshippers must worship in the Spirit and in truth." (*John* 4:24) For the one we worship is a living God who is present among us and is moving actively on earth to fulfil His kingdom purposes. The Holy Spirit, Spirit of God, Holy Lord and His angels are with me. Our Holy God knows the past, present and future: everything we have ever done or will do. My heart was aching and my spirit was in pain, as God convicted me about my past sins. But the Holy Spirit constantly reminds me that I am blessed by God. Hallelujah!

I heard the voice of God saying to me: "Research", "Alone, alone, alone", "This is your church", and "Fast". Our Holy God is real, living, supernatural and powerful. He is LORD Almighty. The Spirit of God knows everything, down to the very littlest detail. I did not know how to write or read, how to read the Bible or pray; but I learnt the Gospel directly from the Holy Spirit and received from Him knowledge that cannot be found in textbooks. He talked to me about many things and gave me insights into people's behavior. As it says in the Bible,

"Silver or gold I do not have, but what I do have I give you. In the name of Jesus Christ of Nazareth..."

Acts 3:6

I received holy wisdom and specific instructions from God, telling me how to set up the Spirit of God Christian Church: the rules and regulations governing the way the church would be run; how He wanted the church services to be conducted; the kinds of ministries the church would have; the people who would make up the congregation; the pastors and preachers who would minister to these people; the place of worship; the physical arrangements and design of the church; and the acceptable ways to obtain funds for the church, one of which would be through the publication and sales of this book.

All profits from the sales of this book will go to the Spirit of God Christian Church Fund. This is how the church will be financially supported, as God has commanded me not to accept donations from people. He used the word "soup" to warn me that I would get into "hot soup" if I were to accept donations. As I have explained earlier, God uses everyday items and bodily gestures to communicate with me. Soup, for example, represents trouble ahead, and is God's way of warning me about potential problems so that I can avoid them.

All of this was from God; I depended entirely on Him, on His holy wisdom, vision and plans for the Church. I was full of joy, as I enjoyed the favor of the LORD. The Holy Spirit told me that God would "open the doors sharp" (meaning, in a wonderful way) for this church to be planted. I received holy wisdom from our Holy God, to employ a secretary to run the Church and to rent premises at the Bible House for church services. The church services would be conducted in both English and Chinese.

I also received holy wisdom from God as to who I could get to preach at the church services—Bible School students preparing to enter the ministry and overseas missionaries on short stopovers in Singapore. (By the way, the Spirit of God really loves these missionaries!)

I received further holy wisdom from the Holy Spirit, to reach out to Permanent Residents and foreigners in Singapore, as well as tourists visiting our country; the Church would be ministering to these people, but Singaporeans are also welcome to join us. All are welcome to volunteer their services at the various ministries in the Church. The Holy Spirit also encourages visitors to come to the Church for daily worship throughout the weekdays, in addition to attending services on weekends. Visitors coming for prayer or worship can bring along a stalk of rose as a symbol of their love for God, as they draw closer to the Spirit of God.

Worshippers will pray in tongues. They will all bow down to our Lord Jesus Christ and to our Holy God and to the Spirit of God during services. They will sing worship songs and receive visions from God. The Spirit of God loves to have worshippers swing and sway their bodies in a supernatural way, as they worship wholeheartedly in spirit, soul and body.

People who come to our services will experience the greatest presence on earth of our Holy God's kingdom. They will lift up their hearts and their hands, and worship the LORD in Spirit and in truth. As it says in the Bible:

"God is spirit, and his worshippers must worship in the Spirit and in truth."

John 4:24 (NIV)

I also received a vision from the Lord that this Church is to serve as a model for other churches which will be planted around the world. Tourists and foreign workers who visit my church will return home and plant churches in their own countries, using my church as a model. These churches will be a legacy for those who come after us—for it is God's will that they should be passed on from generation to generation.

CHAPTER 9

Obeying God—Even when I Am in Tears

$\mathcal{G}$ od called me to write this book. Initially, I almost gave up because there were already so many good books in the market; but the Holy Spirit commanded me to obey, saying it was "His will" for me to write the book. Without His help, I would not have been able to do so; but God reminded me of many miraculous incidents I had already forgotten, so that they could be included in the book.

Where God commands, we must obey; for obedience is better than even the most extravagant sacrifice.

> "Has the Lord as much pleasure in your... sacrifices
> as in your obedience? Obedience is far better than

sacrifice. He is much more interested in your listening to him…"

1 Samuel 15:22 (TLB)

Once, when I was spending a few days at home, tears kept running down my face. I could sense the holy presence of God surrounding me. As I watched sermons on the internet, many times there were tears in my eyes. God's Spirit spoke to me, telling me that the Holy Spirit was present. I began to record down all that the Holy Spirit had done in my life. Although in the natural I had a bad memory, I started to recall incidents that I had long forgotten.

Memories kept flashing into my mind, clear and fresh as if the events had just taken place. The memories stayed in my mind until I had recorded everything down. (As I am not computer-savvy, I did an oral recording that was later transcribed by my daughter into written form.) It was the Holy Spirit who had worked this miracle, so that I could recall all the testimonies He wanted me to share with readers in my book.

As I embarked on writing the book, God showed me an image of tears and told me in advance that I would be writing the book "in tears". He did it to prepare me for the ordeal ahead of me. And it really happened just like He said. I am not fluent in English, so I struggled to find the right words to describe my spiritual experiences. I didn't know how to spell the words, and I couldn't write grammatical sentences.

I tell you the truth, I have not held a pen for decades until I started writing this book. From the time I was young until now that I am in my golden years, I have never written anything in my whole life, so I didn't know anything at all about writing a book. I cried over every word. It was painfully slow-going; it took me many hours just to write and rewrite, and then to check through the pages over and over again for mistakes I had made.

It was a very tough time for me. But I persisted because it was God's command to me to write this book. He gave me the strength to go on. God gives power to the weak. He made a way for me, where there seemed to be no way. Many times, the Holy Spirit would give me the words to write, or He would tell me to replace certain words I had written with more appropriate or powerful ones that He would give to me.

Slowly, the words became more and more until they grew into pages and the pages increased in number. The Holy Spirit kept reminding me of more and more testimonies to share, so much so that the number of pages kept on growing: at first, it was 10 pages; then the 10 became 20, increased to 30, and hit 40 pages—and still the memories kept pouring in, long-forgotten events that I would not have been able to recall on my own. Finally, the whole recording was completed at

60 pages of raw notes, to be rewritten into the actual stories for this book. I had begun writing in tears; but as I kept on writing, I began to experience God's peace, hope and joy. It was all God's doing; He alone made it all possible.

All this was done according to the Holy Spirit's timing, as I managed to finish the oral recording in time for my daughter to begin transcribing it just after she had passed her final-year university exams. What's more, she was able to complete the whole transcription before she got a job and started work!

While the work of writing and transcribing the book was going on, there was one occasion when God told me to check the transcript of my testimonies on the laptop. I had never used a laptop before and thought that I would have difficulties with it. But I obeyed. Wonderful! When I sat down, the laptop was already switched on and ready for me! All I had to do was simply to press the "up" and "down" buttons to read the contents of my book.

The Holy Spirit also showed me how I was to sell the book; I saw a vision of it being sold at a magazine stall. I also intend to sell the book online and to print flyers and banners advertising the book as well as the Spirit of God Christian church. The Holy Spirit has told me that this book is "salt" for the world—meaning that, like salt, it will benefit people, as their eyes will be opened to how they too can experience the Spirit of God moving actively in their lives.

As it says in the Bible:

> "You are the salt of the earth; but if the salt loses
> its flavor, how shall it be seasoned? It is then good
> for nothing but to be thrown out and trampled
> underfoot by men."
>
> *Matthew 5:13 (NKJV)*

Jesus, before I came to know you, I did not know that you cared so much for me. Now that I am saved, I am not ashamed to share the Gospel, although I did not even know how to write or where to start or what to do; but the Spirit of God gave me grace and holy wisdom. Therefore I rejoice that God's Spirit is with me and keeps me close to Him.

CHAPTER 10

Signs and Wonders from the Spirit of God

he Spirit of God never sleeps. He watches over me when I sleep. God's Spirit would wake me up whenever spirits came into my home. One night I woke up at midnight to see a spirit touching my nose. I called out, "LORD!" and the spirit disappeared.

The Spirit of God often appears to me as a transparent image in the form of a person, and we would talk together about many things.

God has opened my eyes and ears to discern the spirit realm. Things unseen and unheard by the physical senses, I have seen and heard with my spiritual eyes and ears. Everywhere I go, I see many people manifesting "cursed lights" inside them. A cursed light is a spirit living inside a human being, and it has a voice that speaks out of the person's body. I can hear the cursed light's voice talking to me, but the person and others around him will not be able to do so.

On another occasion, the Spirit of God woke me up at midnight. I started to pray in tongues. My voice sounded hoarse, as if I had a sore throat, but I continued to pray. A few nights later, God's Spirit again woke me up. I heard a voice praying in tongues. It sounded exactly like me when I was praying with a sore throat. God's Spirit opened my eyes to see a spirit praying in my living room.

Sometimes, when I am talking to a friend, I would smell a sweet fragrance that seems to be emanating, not from any physical object, but from the presence of the Holy Spirit. This is a supernatural aroma that can come from various sources. The Bible also refers to it on several occasions, such as the following:

"For on My holy mountain, on the mountain height of Israel," says the Lord God, "there all the house of Israel, all of them in the land, shall serve Me; there I will accept them, and there I will require your offerings and the first fruits of your sacrifices, together with all your holy things.

"I will accept you as a sweet aroma when I bring you out from the peoples and gather you out

of the countries where you have been scattered;
and I will be hallowed in you before the Gentiles."

Ezekiel 20: 40-41 (NKJV)

Now thanks be to God who always leads us in
triumph in Christ, and through us diffuses the
fragrance of His knowledge in every place.

For we are to God the fragrance of Christ
among those who are being saved and among those
who are perishing.

To the one we are the aroma of death leading
to death, and to the other the aroma of life leading
to life. And who is sufficient for these things?

For we are not, as so many, peddling the word
of God; but as of sincerity, but as from God, we
speak in the sight of God in Christ.;

2 Corinthians 2:14-17 (NKJV)

Many times, too, as I walk along the streets, I begin to smell
a familiar smell associated with my previous church. I look
around me, but there is nothing that could have caused that
particular smell. Then I begin to realize that it is the Holy
Spirit who is supernaturally creating the smell to remind me
of my previous church.

Once, I was on my way to see a doctor when I suddenly felt faint. I quickly sat down on the grass. At the time, I was suffering from diarrhea due to food poisoning. The Spirit of God opened my eyes to see a spirit pointing towards heaven. He was silently telling me that he was from heaven.

On another occasion, when I was visiting my father in hospital, I saw a spirit with food in its mouth, chewing vigorously.

On a separate occasion,, I was at a Traditional Chinese Medicine (TCM) clinic (I wasn't going for treatment there, just checking out their fees). The Spirit of God showed me the word "bread" out of nowhere. I went back to the place to look for bread.

One day, the Spirit of God moved my hand to cover my mouth; this means, "Don't talk" — that is, "Keep this matter a secret." Then He revealed to me that a member of my family had sinned against the Holy Spirit. As it says in the Bible:

> "He who is not with Me is against Me, and he who
> does not gather with Me scatters abroad. Therefore I
> say to you, every sin and blasphemy will be forgiven
> men, but the blasphemy against the Spirit will not
> be forgiven men.

Anyone who speaks a word against the Son of
Man, it will be forgiven him; but whoever speaks
against the Holy Spirit, it will not be forgiven him,
either in this age or in the age to come."

Matthew 12:30-32 (NKJV)

The Holy Spirit said that this was a very serious matter, but
I was not to talk to this family member about it. So I obeyed
the Holy Spirit and kept quiet.

The Spirit of God has opened my spiritual eyes to see
spirits talking with one another; to see an elderly man
sitting in the sky and blowing a flute, as he floated across
the sky. The Spirit of God has opened my eyes to see, in the
atmosphere, many images of people's faces (these are faces of
real people, such as my family, friends and famous people).

While taking a shower, dead cells started coming out
of my back in a supernatural way, as I sensed the presence
of God.

Once I was climbing up a ladder when I suddenly saw,
on top of the ladder, a bright light. On another occasion,
while in the course of delivering a document, I saw to my
surprise that the consignment note I had taken back from the
client had changed from white to blue; and that was when
I again saw a bright light!

One day, I brought my dog to the veterinary clinic to be
treated for a wound. While driving home from the clinic, I

suddenly saw a spirit in the form of a woman. She was sitting beside me, pressing on the dog's wound. The dog barked once. I asked my daughter, who was with me, whether she had pressed on the dog's wound, and she said no.

Once, I was praying in tongues throughout the day, from 10 am till 5 pm. As I prayed, I was amazed to see the hairs on both my hands stand on end and begin to move in waves by themselves.

I saw a vision in the air; it was a vision of praying hands. I had a poster made, with a picture of those praying hands on it, together with quotations from my testimony. I could not put too many words on the plaque due to its limited space; but I still had a lot to say, so I have put my whole testimony into this book.

I wanted to have a cross made of marble with these words engraved on it: "Holy presence of God" in English and "Spirit of God Omnipresent Omnipotent" in Chinese. I worked on the computer, drawing up the design for the cross, and gave the design to the craftsmen who were making the cross for me. When they had completed the job, I displayed this Holy Cross in my home. It was a white marble cross with a red lining that ran all around the outer edge of the cross.

One night, at midnight, I saw that the red outer lining of the cross was flashing supernaturally. It normally does not shine in this way, but that night it kept on shining dazzlingly. I realized that God wanted to draw my attention to something about that cross. I checked on my computer and found that one of the Chinese words in my design had been missed out by the craftsmen; one word was missing from the marble cross! Nevertheless, the Spirit of God often uses that cross to speak to me.

On one occasion, I was facing the marble cross and looking at the Chinese words on it. I called out, "Spirit of God!" in Chinese, and the Spirit of God appeared to me. I will be putting this marble cross in the church that I am setting up, as I mentioned in Chapter 8 of this book.

CHAPTER 11

Snakes and Cursed Lights:
a Warning about Evil People

This is a true story that I witnessed with my own eyes: I saw a cell leader in my former church change into an evil man when he went against his pastor. This cell leader knew the Bible well, but he used Scripture—and even worship songs—for his own purposes. He challenged the pastor's stand on a particular matter, but the pastor stood upon his authority and told him, "This is the law." The cell leader insisted on fighting with the pastor over the issue, but the pastor refused to be drawn into the argument.

This cell leader had a "cursed light" (evil spirit) in him. If you don't like people with "cursed lights" (those with evil spirits in them), they will attack you and try to destroy you. When they talk, the best thing to do is to just keep quiet. The

Spirit of God said that everyone on earth is either for God or the devil. Evil people are heartless; they have no feelings or love for anyone but themselves. They cannot relate to others and they live only for themselves. They harden their hearts and refuse to listen to you; but *you* must listen to them. They reject what you say and try to block you from carrying out your plans. But in God there is freedom. Evil people do not like love, joy or peace.

> A good man out of the good treasure of his heart brings forth good; and an evil man out of the evil treasure of his heart brings forth evil. For out of the abundance of the heart his mouth speaks.
>
> *Luke 6:45 (NKJV)*

Evil people put on a false front of goodness to hide their true nature and hidden agenda. They are like wolves in sheep's clothing. The Holy Spirit said to me that evil people want to take away everything I have and destroy God's plans. The Bible has already warned us about such people:

> They come to you in sheep's clothing, but inwardly they are ferocious wolves. By their fruit you will recognize them.
>
> *Matthew 7: 15-16*

I have seen people close to me turning to evil. To begin with, I never had any problems with them; but when they became evil, they turned against me. Unaware of the change in them or the threat they posed to me, I continued to trust them.

Evil people will find your weakest points and use them against you. They will find a way to get close to you for their own evil purposes. First, they start by getting to know you well. Then they gain your trust by helping you. They show care and concern for you and then—suddenly, without any warning, they will make trouble for you. Their mindset is to serve the evil kingdom. Their lives are given over to stealing, killing and destroying, and their lives are controlled by evil. They talk with curses on their lips, and they live under a curse.

Evil people are connected with one another; they have eyes and ears everywhere, to tell them where you are going and what you are doing. They look for easy targets—for example, people with problems—whom they can get to join their evil kingdom.

> Love must be sincere. Hate what is evil; cling to
> what is good.
>
> *Romans 12:9*

The Spirit of God reveals to me what people are saying behind my back. I can catch, supernaturally out of the air, the very words they speak (just like what happened in *2 Kings 6*, where Elisha knew what the king of Syria was saying privately in his own bedroom)—for example, someone was telling another person that there was nothing good for me and talking about other matters as well. *Thank you very much.*

> Now the king of Syria was making war against Israel; and he consulted with his servants, saying, "My camp will be in such and such a place." And the man of God sent to the king of Israel, saying, "Beware that you do not pass this place, for the Syrians are coming down there."
>
> Then the king of Israel sent someone to the place of which the man of God had told him. Thus he warned him, and he was watchful there, not just once or twice.
>
> Therefore the heart of the king of Syria was greatly troubled by this thing; and he called his servants and said to them, "Will you not show me which of us is for the king of Israel?"
>
> And one of his servants said, "None, my lord, O king; **but Elisha, the prophet who is in Israel, tells the king of Israel the words that you speak in your bedroom."**
>
> *2 Kings 6: 8-12 (NKJV)*

The Holy Spirit tells me He has "tightened evil snake ghosts", meaning that He has prevented these evil people from harming me. The Spirit of God told me that there is pure evil everywhere today, in human beings and in the atmosphere. He has cautioned me that these evil people are big liars with powerful lying tongues; they never stand for Christ. Only those who stand for Christ and His Holy Spirit are true Christians. God told me not to talk to these "evil snakes"; that it is not worth my while to talk to them.

> "You snakes! You brood of vipers! How will you
> escape being condemned to hell?"
>
> *Matthew 23:33*

I have seen, right in front of me, human beings talking to a "cursed light" (an Angel of Light, evil spirit, or devil). The Spirit of God said to me that evil people listen to "cursed lights" and they have assignments from the Evil One. Because of the love of money, they have become evil. They have already lost their original human nature, and now they live in a purely evil way. As Jesus said, "[T]hey don't know what they are doing." (*Luke 23:34, NLT*)

There are some people who profess to be Christians, yet they love these "cursed lights". I once led a man to accept Christ as his Savior. He got baptized, joined a church cell group, was active in the church ushering ministry, helped the weak and went to church services regularly. Then I discovered he had put an idol in my van (I ran a courier service, and he was the deliveryman and driver of the van). When questioned, he replied that he was being secretly "monitored" by the evil kingdom (I don't know why).

There is no other way. If we want to live for Christ, we have to take up our cross and follow Him (*Matthew 16: 24-26*). The Bible tells us that nothing can separate us from God's love (*Romans 8:38*). So, choose to invest in heaven. As Jesus Himself has said:

> "No one can serve two masters. Either you will hate the one and love the other, or you will be devoted to the one and despise the other. You cannot serve both God and money."
>
> *Luke 16:13*

Some people believe that pain and problems come from "cursed lights" (evil spirits or the Evil One). It is true. The Spirit of God told me that it was a cursed light that was causing my body to be in pain and pulling out my teeth. But the Holy Spirit strengthens me with His supernatural power. Once, I felt a pain in my leg. There was no reason for it, as I had not injured myself in any way. I kicked away the pain from the cursed light, and it was gone!

Once, while I was having fish for dinner, I felt a sudden pain in my mouth. A small fishbone was poking into my gums. The Holy Spirit appeared to me (I saw His image) and said that the fishbone had been put there by a "cursed light" and that He would handle the problem for me. He did, and the fishbone miraculously disappeared without my having to do anything about it!

On another occasion, I asked the Spirit of God why I was "walking in the valley"—meaning, why I was facing so many troubles in my life at the time. He replied that those troubles were sent by a "cursed light". But our Holy God works all things out for my good. As it says in the Bible:

> And we know that God causes everything to work together for the good of those who love God and are called according to his purpose for them.
>
> *Romans 8:28 (NLT)*

CHAPTER 12

How the Holy Spirit Speaks to Me

The Holy Spirit speaks to me using everyday objects, common images and words, and simple bodily movements; each of these conveys a different and specific meaning. Below, I have given examples of each mode of communication. When the Spirit of God speaks, the message—in whatever form it comes—is always fresh, lively and full of supernatural power.

Using Objects to Communicate

This is the most common mode of communication. The Holy Spirit often draws my attention to an actual, physical object, and sometimes He will even turn my head around to look at it. For example, when He shows me a showerhead, He is calling me to pray. He will also show me what He wants me to pray for. When He shows me a piece of soap—which sounds like "soup"—He means "in hot soup"; that is, there are problems ahead or someone is in deep trouble.

Sometimes it is quite obvious what an object stands for. An umbrella, for instance, means "protection"; a money plant means "money"; a close-circuit camera means "eyes"; and fruit mean "the fruit of the Spirit". At other times, the object is used to convey a deeper and more specific message. For example, an electrical wire means "to be on fire for God"; and a wall plug means "plug in and act on it"; that is, to plug into the power of God and take action in a particular matter. When it is a power point with the switch in the "on" position, it means "take action"; if it is switched off, it means "relax; don't do anything".

A water pipe with a cover on it means that the Holy Spirit will "cover" (that is, protect) me when I am engaged in spiritual warfare with the enemy. A water-pipe joint, on the other hand, means that He will join in the fight with me and there will be a breakthrough. And when the Holy Spirit shows me a water tap, He is focusing on the word "tap" (as in tapping one's EZ-Link card at the train station entry and exit gantries, which allows the system to keep tabs on your travel movements) and telling me that He is keeping tabs on me.

When the Holy Spirit shows me a blank television screen that lights up, He means that "in the darkness you can see the Light". Light shining through the louvered glass panels of a small toilet window means that certain paragraphs of text (for example, in a book or periodical) will enlighten readers and cause them to see God. A clothespin—the kind that clips clothes together—means that someone has "clicked" (which sounds like "clipped") on a link directing them to my testimony on the internet.

The Holy Spirit often uses words that sound alike. For example, when He shows me a knife, He is telling me that someone—a particular person — is nice (which sounds like "knife"). A rusty lock, on the other hand, means "this is a nasty person". ("Nasty" sounds like "rusty"—get it?) A door means "this is a running dog"—in other words, a sycophant; but a ceiling fan means "this is a friend". ("Door" is close in sound to "dog", and "fan" to "friend".)

When the Holy Spirit shows me a cupboard handle, He means that He will handle a particular problem for me. When it is a shoe cabinet handle, it means that a particular organization is "handled" or run by "rats" (nasty people). And when the Holy Spirit shows me a shoe, He means "fool"; that is, He is warning me that someone is fooling me or about to fool me; or it can also mean that the person is a fool. A shirt collar, on the other hand, means "scholar"—indicating that this is a learned person.

When the Holy Spirit shows me a rice cooker, He is telling me, "This is Holy God's rice bowl"—that is, something extremely important or valuable to God, and dear to His heart. When He turns my head to look at the clock, it means that an event will take place "in God's timing". A hook means "hope"; and a document file means that He is telling me to "keep it"; for example, to file a piece of information away for future use. And when He shows me a packet of seeds, it means that I will be getting many new clients for my business. True! One by one, the clients kept coming to me!

A road sign, of an adult holding a child's hand, means that the Holy Spirit will hold my hand and walk with me. The Holy Spirit often uses road signs and other common signs to communicate with me. Here are some of them:

❖ A Pedestrian Crossing sign means that someone wants to "crossover";

❖ A "No Littering" sign means "don't throw away God's blessings" or "don't reject God's blessings";

❖ A "No Smoking" sign means "no spreading this piece of news around; don't talk about it";

❖ A hairdresser's "hair perm" sign means someone has been "burnt" or hurt by a past experience;

❖ A "No Parking" sign means "no barking" — that is, do not talk garrulously, like a dog barking noisily;

❖ A "No Dogs Allowed" sign means "no running dogs"; that is, "don't have anything to do with sycophants".

The Holy Spirit also gives me insights into people and information about them that I would not have known on my own. Here are some examples:

❖ A bird means "burst"; that is, someone can't hold it in anymore and is about to burst (for example, because of some strong emotion or exciting news);

❖ A box means "this is the boss";

❖ A button says "this is a pastor";

❖ A cat means "someone is scared";

❖ A key ring means "key person(s)"; for example, the board of directors or senior management of an organization;

❖ A lamp post or wall lamp means "a lamb" — that is, a good person

❖   A paper bag means "a batch of people";

❖   A shaving razor means that someone (a particular person) is safe and sound;

❖   A screw being tightened means someone is "tightening" his grip or control on another person;

❖   A sound speaker system refers to a "preacher";

❖   Paint means "pain" — that is, someone is in pain.

Sometimes the Holy Spirit uses everyday objects to show me what He wants me to do or to tell me about future events. The following are a few examples:

❖   A bottle of "Axe Brand" medicated oil means that the Holy Spirit wants me to take up cudgels and fight or protest against something;

❖   A bottle of Blanco (eraser fluid) means "don't write anything now";

❖   A chair means "better check this out";

❖   An eraser means "there is trouble ahead";

❖ A pencil or piece of paper means "write";

❖ A pendulum means "rise";

❖ A piece of tissue paper means "someone will do you a great favor".

Communicating through Images

Sometimes I receive visions and images in my mind when the Holy Spirit wants to communicate with me. For example, when He gives me an image of a postage stamp, it means that He wants me to take a stand on a particular matter. When He shows me a picture of weighing scales (the old-fashioned type, with two balancing pans), He is talking about justice.

A dove refers to the Holy Spirit and an image of angels means that there are angels present. A vision of an arrow means "shoot" — but not literally with an arrow; rather, it means "to shoot out words in a forthright way; to speak out strongly". A square shape—whether big or small—means "share sharp"; that is, to share the Gospel or my testimony deeply and in an excellent way with others.

On one occasion, the Holy Spirit showed me a vision of a lock on a bicycle wheel, to warn me that evil men were out to "lock" me up (that is, stop me) so that I could not do God's will, just like a bicycle that is unable to move if its wheels have been locked.

Revelations about People

Apart from using objects to give me insights into people, the Holy Spirit also gives me revelations about them by making me feel what they are feeling. When the Holy Spirit makes my heart beat very fast— in a way that is not natural, but supernaturally by His power—He is revealing to me that someone is scared. When He makes me feel a pain in my feet, again not naturally but by His supernatural power, it is a revelation from Him that someone is in pain.

Sometimes when I meet people, the Holy Spirit will reveal their true feelings to me, even when they try to hide them. When a person does not really like something (for example, a suggestion I make), the Holy Spirit will show me an unlighted bulb; but He will show me a lighted bulb if the person is happy.

Bodily Movements and Gestures

While I am fully in control of my own physical body, there are times when the Holy Spirit moves a part of my body—

usually one of my hands or legs—to give me a revelation about someone. For example, when He wants to show me that a particular person is feeling fearful, He moves my hand to scratch my ribs. When He is talking about what is in someone's heart—that is, what they are really like inside or what they are feeling—the Holy Spirit often moves my hand to scratch my chest.

When the Holy Spirit moves my fingers to dig my ears, He is telling me that someone has pricked up his or her ears (or has sharp hearing) and is listening attentively. When He moves my hand to scratch my head, He is indicating to me a particular person who heads an organization or is in charge of a certain project. And when the Spirit of God moves me to scratch my hand, He is informing me that someone "hangs" ("hand" sounds like "hang") — meaning, the person is in trouble or is paralyzed with fear because of a serious problem, much like a computer can't function anymore if it "hangs".

When the Spirit of God lifts my finger up to touch my eyebrow, He is telling me, "Holy God's rice bowl"—meaning that a particular matter is extremely important to God or close to His heart. And when the He moves my finger to plug my ear, He is telling me to listen attentively. Sometimes, the Holy Spirit makes my whole body go still; this is His signal to me to pause because He wants me to see something or He wants to reveal something to me.

When the Spirit of God moves my finger to rub my nose, He means that a particular person is from God. But if He lifts my finger to touch my lip, it means that what someone is saying is not from God —for example, a pastor preaching a sermon. It is only the person's own words (even though he may be claiming that it is a message from God). And when the Spirit of God moves my hand to touch the hairs on my chin, He is telling me that someone I am thinking of is safe.

When the Spirit of God moves my hand to make a clenched fist, with my thumb sticking out, and moves me to flick my thumb, He is telling me that a recent event is blessed and good. How blessed or good it is can be determined by the sound produced when my thumb is flicked.

When the Spirit of God knows that a blessing is coming my way, He would move my fingers to pinch my nose. When He wants to tell me that someone knows something about me, He would move my fingers to touch my nose sideways; if the person has important information about me, He would move my fingers to touch the middle of my nose. Breathing in deeply through the nose means there is a tough situation looming up ahead.

When the Holy Spirit raises my finger to touch my neck, He is telling me about "people in the nest" ("neck" and "nest" sound alike). This phrase refers to people who gather together for their own evil purposes and to talk maliciously about others, like a nest or brood of vipers. As it says in the Bible:

> You brood of vipers, how can you who are evil say anything good? For the mouth speaks what the heart is full of.
>
> *Matthew 12:34*

> They make their tongues as sharp as a serpent's; the poison of vipers is on their lips.
>
> *Psalm 140:3*

Words with Special Meanings

Sometimes the Holy Spirit speaks to me in words. Each word He uses holds a special meaning; for example, when He says "rest", He is telling me to be at peace and not to keep waiting anxiously for an event to happen.

The Holy Spirit often uses the word "sharp" to mean "knowledge that penetrates deeper into one's heart"; or "to seek or receive deeper knowledge, insight and discernment about a matter"; or "to do something excellently". For example, the Holy Spirit tells me that those who do me a favor "sharp" (meaning, in an excellent way) will be covered and have rest from trouble.

When the Spirit of God tells me that evil men want to "crucify" someone, He means that those people intend to destroy a particular person (who can be me or another person). The Spirit of God often tells me, too, that these evil people have set out to "crucify" (that is, destroy) God's work.

An "ape" or an "eight" means a person who prefers to please men rather than God. "Lamb", on the other hand, means someone who belongs to God's kingdom. "Ghost" means a spy (informer), or an evil person, or someone from the evil kingdom. For example, I have heard God's voice (an actual voice coming out of the air) telling me that it was not worth talking to "evil snake ghosts"—that is, it was not worth my time talking to devious schemers who were working for Satan.

Some other words that the Holy Spirit uses to communicate with me are:

- ❖ "Serve the Lord" means "serve the lost";

- ❖ "Comfort" means "a flock of sheep" — that is, the congregation in a church;

- ❖ "Central" means "sense it's real" — that is, it's genuine, not a fake;

❖ "Valley" means "trouble" (this word is used in the same sense as in *Psalm 23:4*, which talks about walking through the darkest valley);

❖ "Fish" means "available person"—that is, someone who is not a believer but is available for me to lead to Christ;

❖ "Chew" means to "keep chewing on and on" or to meditate on God's Word (the Bible);

❖ "Cursed Light" means an Angel of Light (that is, the devil) or an evil spirit. The Holy Spirit has told me that this "Cursed Light" wants to destroy God's plans but he is being "tightened" (see meaning below);

❖ "Tighten" means to hold someone tightly to prevent them from doing or saying something—for example, when the Holy Spirit tells me He has "tightened evil snake ghosts", He means that He has held them back from acting or talking against me. As I mentioned in Chapter 11 above, when people start to say negative things about me, God tightens His hold on them to shut them up.

Communicating with Numbers

Certain numbers convey specific messages from the Holy Spirit. Here are some examples:

- ❖ 00 means "No, no!"

- ❖ 1 means "eyes"

- ❖ 2 means "shoot and hook" or "shoot and hope"; that is, to "shoot" out words forthrightly, in the hope that the hearer is gripped or "hooked" by those words

- ❖ 3 means "heaven, earth and hook/hope"

- ❖ 4 means "false"

- ❖ 5 means "fight"; to challenge someone to a fight

- ❖ 6 means "fight" (see 5 above) and "hook" or "hope" (see 2 above)

- ❖ 8 or "ape" means someone who would rather please men than God

❖ 9 means "nice"

❖ 10 means "hang"

❖ 12 means "dwell"

Statement of Faith of Spirit of God Christian Church (Singapore)

Holy Spirit

We believe that the Holy Spirit was sent from God as life and power for those who believe in Jesus Christ. Through the Holy Spirit, we are transformed in our character and empowered in our services, so that we may be like Christ.

The Bible

We believe that the Bible is God's written Word. It contains all things necessary for salvation, teaches God's will for His world, and has supreme authority for faith, life, and the continuous renewal and reform of the Church.

Salvation

We believe that we are saved from our sins and reconciled to God only through believing and accepting what Jesus Christ has done for us on the cross. It is not by our efforts or merit, but it is a gift from God.

The Church

We believe:

❖ That the Church is the Body of Christ, whose members believe in Jesus Christ and acknowledge His headship. They are joined together by the Holy Spirit;

❖ The Scriptures, both Old and New Testaments, to be the inspired Word of God, without error in the original writings, the complete revelation of His will for the salvation of men and the divine and final authority for Christian faith and Life;

❖   In one God, creator of all things, infinitely perfect and eternally existing in three persons: Father, Son and Holy Spirit;

❖   That Jesus Christ is true God and true Man, having been conceived of the Holy Spirit and born of the Virgin Mary. He died on the cross, a sacrifice for our sins according to the Scriptures. Further, He arose bodily from the dead and ascended into heaven, where, at the right hand of the Majesty on High, He is now our High Priest and Advocate;

❖   That the ministry of the Holy Spirit is to glorify the Lord Jesus Christ and, during this age, to convict men, regenerate the believing sinner, and indwell, guide, instruct and empower the believer for godly living and service;

❖   That the true Church is composed of all such persons who, through saving faith in Jesus Christ, have been regenerated by the Holy Spirit and are united together in the Body of Christ, of which He is the Head.

APPENDIX II

Spirit of God Performs Miracles

Spirit God open eye show name card in van. Spirit God show water pipe dusty. Spirit God show plastic clothespin often speak in silent which means clip. Spirit God tell in silent show soap which means problem. Spirit God show Holy Spirit sign speak in silent which means Holy Spirit presence. Spirit God tell in silent like or don't like people. Spirit God tell in silent man of rush often. Spirit God tell in silent Holy God timing. Spirit God tell in silent cursed light. Spirit God call in silent to sell van. Spirit God call in silent to listen in presence.

Spirit God open spiritual eye seen unseen thing. Spirit God open spiritual eye seen spiritual person pray. Spirit God tell in silent before me in the presence. Spirit God open spiritual eye seen spiritual person point at heaven. Spirit

God know everything tell in silent. Spirit God appeared tell in silent in toilet about church fund. Spirit God tell in silent what you want self-service.

Spirit God tell in silent trust Holy God. Spirit God tell in silent evil man take away Holy God plan. Spirit God tell in silent online sermon pray in tongue is for me. Spirit God in me relationship deeper. Spirit God call in silent take Chinese tea. Spirit God with me in battle. Spirit God love overseas missionary. Spirit God tell in silent to write listen online sermon. Spirit God give knowledge and holy wisdom of God. Spirit God open spiritual eye seen bread English words in supernatural way appear out of nowhere.

Spirit God open spiritual eye seen fear no evil act in supernatural way. Spirit God show Angels sign speak in silent. Spirit God often tell in silent tighten. Spirit God tell in silent shoot in the track sharp. Spirit God tell in silent healing. Spirit God will tell in silent not from Holy God. Spirit God tell in silent supernatural tears flow. Spirit God tell in silent share sharp people said. Spirit God tell in silent hang.

Spirit God command in silent pray in tongue roll. Spirit God tell in silent Holy presence of God. Spirit God tell in silent need to go location bible house. Spirit God tell in silent evil man present. Spirit God tell in silent Holy God or evil. Spirit God open spiritual eye seen Holy God disappeared. Spirit God open spiritual eye seen Holy words. Spirit God open spiritual eye seen spirit in room. Spirit God make cough in present.

Spirit God teach what type preaching. Spirit God love body swing see Spirit God Holy spiritually appeared. Spirit God speak in silent powerfully his words. Spirit God cry out with tears solemnly. Spirit God often tell in silent crucify. Spirit God supernatural super power move head and open spiritual eye seen. Spirit God supernatural super power clenched fist with thumb sticking out. Spirit God tell in silent Nick Vujicic. Spirit God command in silent evil.

Turn head round from Spirit God. Bread from Spirit God. Spirit God command in silent his namesake for his people. File which means keep from Spirit God. No running dog from Spirit God. Spirit God turn my head see clock which means Holy God timing. Let us remember Holy presence of God from Spirit God. Spirit God command in silent listen radio.

Lighted bulb from Spirit God put out teeth from Spirit God. Switch on or off from Spirit God Spirit God command in silent. Mercy shall follow me. Spirit God command in silent paragraph. Supernatural super power stop write pen cannot write which means don't write unacceptable words stop by Spirit God. Spirit God used fingers to touch beard, which means safe. Spirit God picking nose, which means find out something. Spirit God scratched hands, which means hang.

Spirit God likes listen news, like degree people, Spirit God tell in silent sharp. Mortarboard/graduate hat which means degree or degree sharp. Spirit God love gospel and worshipping body swing. Believe this is bringing knowledge to life. beginning scared, Spirit God appeared tell in silent from Psalm poster fear no evil Spirit God appeared tell in silent from Psalm poster before me in the presence which means Spirit God inside body already before accept Christ.

Spirit God command in silent all the days of my life. Spirit God knows thoughts and responds to it immediately. Spirit God kept on talking about gospel even if don't understand. Crucify from Spirit God. Spirit God open spiritual eye seen spiritual person many other spirit. Spirit God act in supernatural way yawn tell in silent tired or don't want. Spirit God speak in silent protection over our family obedience better than sacrifice.

Spirit God open spiritual eye seen an elderly sitting in sky blow flute moved across sky. Spirit God teach sermon categorize. Spirit God show money plant. Spirit God supernatural super power wearing cross necklace dropped. Spirit God supernatural super power lift up finger touch nose eye brow lip face ear head. Spirit God tell in silent show wall got small hole. Spirit God kept reminding track broken.

Spirit God tell in silent about many things feedback about people reaction. Spirit God super power dynamic marvelous invisible. Spirit God let me know good or bad problem and other. Spirit God appeared tell in silent call him Spirit God. Anything from Spirit God perfect. Heart begging is to see the nation worship Spirit God. The HOLY LORD, The shepherd and his people from Spirit God. Spirit God command in silent all the days of my life.

Spirit God command in silent body half is Spirit God half is own hand and leg gestures talked in silent to each other. Spirit God often tell in silent evil men crucify. Spirit God tell in silent cursed light put pain in body pull out teeth. Spirit God turn head seen clock mean Holy God timing. Spirit God tell in silent cursed light want to take away Holy God plan. Spirit God tell in silent about evil enemy man of rusty and crucify.

Spirit God omnipresence omnipotent omniscient. Believe Spirit God in human life. Spirit God appeared I faced Holy cross look at Holy Chinese word call out name Spirit God. Spirit God tell in silent don't promise anything to worshipper. Spirit God appeared command in silent unacceptable donation. Reason soup which means problem. Spirit God tell in silent Holy presence of God. Spirit God open spiritual eye seen vision praying hands. Spirit God appeared presence seen face to face.

Spirit God appeared tell in silent fear no evil many other from Psalm poster. Spirit God supernatural Holy open spiritual eye seen heard Holy God voice speak alone, alone, alone and disappeared image saw Holy God image whole body was still only eye see lady voice . Spirit God tell in silent Holy Spirit presence. Spirit God command in silent the HOLY LORD the shepherd of his people.

Spirit God use hand cover mouth which means don't talk. Spirit God supernatural super power lift up finger touch eyebrow which means Holy God rice bowl. The Spirit God lives in me and commands in silent my body while fully in control of my own movements I nevertheless move according to his leading living lively actively in my life. Spirit God woke up to listen preaching on the internet.

At night was in master bedroom lie down on bed supernatural head turn one round seen up electrical wire track a bit scared and Spirit God tell in silent all go in to cupboard long sleeve and short sleeve hang Spirit God which means track are broken. Receive from Holy God Spirit God Christian Church. Spirit God kept reminding track broken tell in silent act in supernatural way. Spirit God opened eyes seen spirits talking in silent each other see spiritual person and others over time.

Spirit God opened eyes seen an elderly man sitting in sky blow flute moved across sky. Spirit God call in silent cut hair drink cold and hot healthy food many other praise the HOLY LORD faithful LORD. Spirit God released supernatural power wore cross necklace dropped on floor checked nothing wrong. Hearing from the HOLY LORD powerfully abide in his words. The HOLY LORD cry out with tears solemnly.

Spirit God tell in silent act in supernatural way super power people nose can smell about me.

Spirit God tell in silent cursed light have been tighten. Spirit God supernatural super power lift up finger touch small pimple pain beside nose which means someone checking pain act in supernatural way. Spirit God command in silent paragraphs to see light and Holy God words are sharp. Spirit God act in supernaturally way would categorize them under their respective ministries online.

Spirit God use gospel object words talk in silent presence living room. Spirit God turned head look money plant in toilet which means our conversation about money act in supernatural way. Spirit God teaching gospel use house hold all kind of object wall got small hole Spirit God tell in silent. Spirit God command in silent his namesake for his people. Holy Spirit command in silent daily office hour for worshipper to worship Spirit God only.

Spirit God call a person ape mean light. Act in supernatural super power my mind often dwell in gospel. Act in supernatural super power my mind keep on chew in gospel. Bible scripture "Let the word of Christ dwell in you richly in all holy wisdom, teaching and admonishing one another in psalms and hymns and spiritual songs, singing with grace in your hearts to the Lord." Colossians 3:16

Nevertheless, of those that chew the cud or have cloven hooves, you shall not eat, such as these: the camel, the hare, and the rock hyrax; for they chew the cud but do not have cloven hooves; they are unclean for you. Deuteronomy 14:7-9.

Receive hearing call Holy God. Spirit God tell in silent evil man crucify which means destroy. Pray or worship can bring along one stalk of rose more close to Spirit God for service. Tighten which means holy god hold a person movement or action or talking. Psalm 46:10: Be still, and know that I am God; I will be exalted among the nations, I will be exalted in the earth!

Revelation 19:15: Now out of His mouth goes a sharp sword, that with it He should strike the nations. And He Himself will rule them with a rod of iron. He Himself treads the winepress of the fierceness and wrath of Almighty God.

Isaiah 40:31: But those who wait on the Holy Lord shall renew their strength; they shall mount up with wings like eagles, they shall run and not be weary, they shall walk and not faint.

Fish which means available person. Neck which means someone in the nest. Spirit God supernatural super power lift finger touch my neck which means someone was in the nest. Sharp which means knowledge deeper in heart. Spirit God tell in silent evil men crucify which means destroy. Spirit God command in silent darkness can see light which means see God bible said Act 26:18 "to open their eyes, in order to turn them from darkness to light, and from the power of Satan to God, that they may receive forgiveness of sins and an inheritance among those who are sanctified by faith in Me."

I receive supernatural super power everywhere many people manifest spiritual idol mean light with voice speak in human body experience Holy God supernatural super power bible scripture "But you shall receive power when the Holy Spirit has come upon you, and you shall be witnesses to me in Jerusalem, and in all Judea and Samaria, and to the end of the earth." Acts 1:8 Hand which means hang. Touch my lip mean my own words. Chew which means chew the God's words on and on. Whole body still which means pause, valley which means trouble.

Holy God is a holy lady with voice speak to me part of angel. Spirit God supernatural super power lift finger touch my lip which means not from Holy God. I was writing the testimony and sit on the chair I don't know why seriously fell on the floor,. The chair was reverse. I feel supernatural super power landing very lightly on the floor and safe. at this moment, I speak out complete writing the testimony. Praise the lord. Holy God appeared is holy lady with voice speak to me part of angel.

Calendar bible words is Holy Spirit talk about my faith walk with the Lord. All act in supernatural way. Holy Spirit appeared talk to me in spiritually form of person image. Spirit God talk to me in spirit form image. I saw a spirit came into my home and ask what happen talk to the Spirit God and

Spirit God answer the spirit said it is the cursed light in the spiritually situation. Mark 5:41 "Holding her hand, he said to her, "Talitha koum," which means "Little girl, get up!""

I was riding the motorbike one of my hand was very numb Spirit God call for pray in tongue the numbness was gone praise the Lord. Presence with means sense. Atmosphere receive heard man voice speak in Chinese 天上无难事最怕有心人."Where there is a will, there is a way".

Because of my Chinese A5 book, Holy Spirit command power to know more with mean reader read to the testimony about God power to know more were go to new lever. Holy Spirit command bringing knowledge to life with means read the testimony know more about Holy God knowledge your faith go to new lever. Spirit God show words over with mean war is over. Holy God said lady voice is Holy God (confirm). Spirit God command reader to file or keep testimony.

Holy Spirit show the letter box window with means people close doors. Holy Spirit command many item show shine light. Holy God tell about spiritually power my hand muscle or place hand together pray for war was moving. Holy Spirit woke me up online sermon bible words for testimony thank you Lord. The book is not only for church fund also share the testimony to the whole world and fulfillment Holy Spirit his will.

Bible said Habbakuk 2:20 but the Lord is in His holy temple is for the name of daily worship. Bible said Luke 10:19

Behold, I give you the authority to trample on serpents and scorpions and over all the power of the enemy and nothing shall by any means hurt you. Bible said Joshua 1:9 for the Lord your God will be with you wherever you go.

I Heard the Voice of
our Holy God

Experience Holy God kingdom super power dynamic marvelous invisible. Obedience better than sacrifice. 1 Samuel 15:22. Atmosphere heard Holy God tell in silent fight matter. Atmosphere heard Holy Spirit command in silent a Chinese bible Matthew scripture 5: 3-10 calendar. Atmosphere heard Holy God step down. Atmosphere heard Holy God voice alone and disappeared. Atmosphere heard Holy God pass business to next generation. Atmosphere heard Holy God give room to girl. Atmosphere heard Holy God no need leave church. Atmosphere heard Holy God voice this is your church.

Atmosphere heard Holy God tithe. Atmosphere heard Holy God true Christian. Atmosphere heard Holy God plant church. Atmosphere heard Holy God don't go down stair eat. Atmosphere heard Holy God cancel personal thing. Atmosphere heard Holy God carrot juice. Atmosphere heard Holy God voice is lady speak. Atmosphere heard Holy God voice not worth to talk. Atmosphere heard Holy God seen vision tell in silent bow down and place hand together pray. Atmosphere heard Holy God worshipping with song in heart. Atmosphere heard Holy God voice and disappeared like throw stone in water spread out. Holy God know with part of body pain. Atmosphere heard the HOLY LORD, The shepherd and his people from Spirit God. Atmosphere heard Spirit God command in silent darkness can see light which means see God Act 26:18 "to open their eyes, in order to turn them from darkness to light, and from the power of Satan to God, that they may receive forgiveness of sins and an inheritance among those who are sanctified by faith in Me".

Atmosphere heard Spirit God command in silent all the days of my life. Atmosphere heard Holy Spirit command in silent this is bringing knowledge to life. Atmosphere heard Spirit God command in silent body half is Spirit God half is own hand and leg gestures talked to each other. Atmosphere heard Spirit God command in silent mercy shall follow me. Atmosphere heard holy wisdom from Holy God ministry for tourists and foreigners. Experience greatest Holy God kingdom lively actively presence on earth Holy Spirit, Spirit God, Angels, Holy God, Holy God words, HOLY LORD with me. Atmosphere heard voice Holy God said not worth talk to evil snake ghosts. Atmosphere heard Holy Spirit tell in silent tighten ghost snake evil. Atmosphere heard Spirit God tell in silent cursed light put pain in body pull out teeth. Atmosphere heard Spirit God tell in silent cursed light want to take away Holy God plan. Atmosphere heard Holy God kingdom tell in silent don't know or forgotten Holy words for The world power Testimony. Atmosphere heard Spirit God in human life. Atmosphere heard Holy Spirit command in silent the New Testament.

Atmosphere heard Spirit God appeared I faced Holy cross look at Holy Chinese word call out name Spirit God. Spirit God command in silent pray in tongue roll. Atmosphere heard Spirit God tell in silent don't promise anything to worshipper. Atmosphere heard Spirit God appeared command in silent unacceptable donation and fund. Reason soup which means problem. Atmosphere heard Holy Spirit command in silent his will Holy book. Atmosphere heard Spirit God tell in silent Holy presence of God.

Atmosphere heard Spirit God appeared tell in silent fear no evil many other from Psalm poster. Atmosphere heard Spirit God tell in silent Holy Spirit presence. Atmosphere heard Spirit God command in silent the HOLY LORD the shepherd of his people. Atmosphere heard Holy God dare spend money for LORD. Atmosphere heard Highly recommended from Holy God. Atmosphere heard Spirit God use hand cover mouth which means don't talk. Atmosphere heard Holy God use laptop check The world power Testimony. Atmosphere heard Holy Spirit command in silent Holy God open door sharp. Atmosphere heard Holy Spirit often to rest room tell in silent about cursed light or Holy God with bowel motion presence situation. Atmosphere heard Holy Spirit call in silent for abide in Holy God supernatural teeth were soft bite. Atmosphere heard Spirit God often don't like or unacceptable and not true presence situation caused fart. Atmosphere heard Holy Spirit call in silent for bible scripture put in The world power Testimony. Atmosphere heard Holy Spirit command in silent gospel lead deliver Holy words how to write. Atmosphere heard Receive holy wisdom from Holy God tithing and true Christian.

Atmosphere heard Holy God use me mightily shine for Jesus around The world. Atmosphere heard Holy God said brother against Holy Spirit. Atmosphere heard Spirit God finger plug in ear which means listen. Atmosphere heard Holy Spirit tell in silent trouble. Atmosphere heard Holy Spirit heal brain return memory receive holy wisdom from Holy God and health. Atmosphere heard receive Holy Spirit command in silent The world power testimony is salt which means "You are the salt of the earth; but if the salt loses its flavor, how shall it be seasoned? It is then good for nothing but to be thrown out and trampled underfoot by me" Matthew 5:13. Atmosphere heard receive holy wisdom from Holy God secretary run church Atmosphere heard receive Holy Spirit command in silent global Atmosphere heard receive Holy Spirit tell in silent God will make a way. Atmosphere heard receive Spirit God tell in silent need to go location bible house. Atmosphere heard receive Holy God voice alone came to pass take more than 10 years to know why. Atmosphere heard Receive from Holy God Spirit God Christian Church. Atmosphere heard receive Spirit God act in supernatural way super power that people nose can smell about me. Atmosphere heard receive Spirit God often tell in silent cursed light been tighten. Atmosphere heard receive from Holy God kingdom which means Holy book. Atmosphere heard receive Pray in tongue for healing spiritually warfare protection or prayer through Holy God with his power welcome Holy Spirit Holy presence supernatural tears flow. Atmosphere heard receive from the truth and the life I am your God. Atmosphere heard Spirit God command in silent his namesake for his people. Atmosphere heard Spirit God command in silent paragraph can see light which means see Holy God. Atmosphere heard receive from Holy God super power, Christian church, interesting to read, research, begging, step down, bible society, act in supernatural way. Atmosphere heard Holy Spirit command in silent share sharp. Atmosphere heard Holy Spirit command in silent rice bowl which means Holy God. Atmosphere heard Holy Spirit command in silent the power you know more. Atmosphere heard Holy Spirit command in silent open wing to fight which means challenging. Atmosphere heard Holy Spirit command in silent shoot go up mean raise. Atmosphere heard Holy Spirit appeared command in silent rice cooker which means Holy God rice bowl. Atmosphere heard Holy God rice bowl which means Holy God. Atmosphere heard Holy Spirit appeared command in silent worship the HOLY LORD in daily office hours. Atmosphere heard Holy Spirit appeared command in silent generation to generation planting new church. Atmosphere heard Spirit God call me in silent to pray in tongue for my hand numbness, at this moment my hand was very numbness was gone. Atmosphere heard Spirit God supernatural super power lift up finger touch eyebrow which means Holy God rice bowl. Atmosphere heard Holy Spirit holy calling open wings to shoot with angels with tears alone and justice. Atmosphere heard Jesus said I am the way the life and the truth. Atmosphere heard Spirit God supernatural super power destroy light bulb dead with sound bulb was on.

HOLY LORD powerful. Marvelous. Receive hearing call Holy God.

Holy Spirit Performs Miracles

*H*oly Spirit show super power invincible. Holy Spirit handle in trouble. Holy Spirit call in silent employ helper. Holy Spirit controlled handphone. Holy Spirit tell in silent do you favour sharp. Holy Spirit tell in silent trouble. Holy Spirit tell in silent God letters without s. Holy Spirit tell in silent hook in is cursed light. Holy Spirit tell in silent track draw line. Holy Spirit tell in silent track close door. Holy Spirit tell in silent war in presence. Holy Spirit sent to toilet. Holy Spirit tell in silent hold don't give.

Holy Spirit tell in silent Holy God open door sharp. Holy Spirit tell in silent face valley. Holy Spirit woke up listen online sermon. Holy Spirit make body itchy. Holy Spirit command in silent generation to generation plant church. Holy Spirit command in silent daily office hour worship the LORD. Holy Spirit command in silent Holy book cover words. Holy Spirit tell in silent evil lock God will. Holy

Spirit tell in silent wait upon the HOLY LORD for church. Holy Spirit is man appeared Holy Spiritually.

Holy Spirit tell in silent open wind pray. Holy Spirit tell in silent open wind shoot. Holy Spirit tell in silent open wind fight. Holy Spirit tell in silent God will make a way. Holy Spirit tell in silent protest. Holy Spirit tell in silent shoot go up. Holy Spirit tell in silent take healthy food. Holy Spirit tell in silent throw everything out you know. Holy Spirit command in silent file which means holy God The world power Testimony. Holy Spirit command in silent The new testament.

Real fresh from Holy Spirit. Abide from Holy Spirit. Spiritually fruit from Holy Spirit. 1.5 drinking bottle from Holy Spirit. Holy Spirit command in silent global. Holy Spirit command in silent see many people face light. The world power Testimony is salt which means "You are the salt of the earth; but if the salt loses its flavor, how shall it be seasoned? It is then good for nothing but to be thrown out and trampled underfoot by me" Matthew 5:13 from Holy Spirit valley from Holy Spirit war + war. Holy Spirit power stop talking control throat. Holy Spirit tell in silent receive power from Holy God. Holy Spirit tell in silent show pack of seed which means many new client obedience better than sacrifice. Holy Spirit tell in silent spiritually fruits. Holy Spirit command in silent this is bringing knowledge to life. Holy Spirit handle warfare trouble attack and many other.

Holy Spirit call in silent to send catholic theology. Holy Spirit supernatural power worshipping wept Holy Spirit super power dynamic. Holy Spirit tell in silent hot soup which means problem marvelous invisible. Holy Spirit talks about many things feedback about people reaction. Holy Spirit tell in silent Nick Vujick speak in church coughed is a light. Holy Spirit command in silent put scripture bible word in testimony anything from Holy Spirit perfect.

Holy Spirit let me know good or bad problem and other. Experience greatest Holy God kingdom lively, actively, presence on earth, Holy Spirit, Spirit God, Angels, Holy God, Holy God words, HOLY LORD with me. Holy Spirit tell in silent tighten ghost snake evil. Holy Spirit tell in silent Holy God were make a wave. Holy Spirit tell in silent ghost will make a wave. Experience Holy Spirit super power dynamic marvelous invincible. Holy Spirit tell in silent fishbone poke in mouth from cursed light Holy Spirit handle fish bone disappeared presence.

Experience Holy Spirit omnipresence omnipotent omniscient. Holy Spirit appeared presence seen face to face. Holy Spirit command in silent his will Holy book. Holy Spirit command in silent Holy God open door sharp. Holy Spirit often to rest room tell in silent about cursed light or Holy God with bowel motion presence situation.

Holy Spirit call in silent for abide in Holy God supernaturally teeth were soft bite. Holy Spirit call in silent for bible scripture put in The world power Testimony. Holy Spirit tell in silent trouble. Holy Spirit heal brain return memory receive holy wisdom from Holy God and health. Holy Spirit appeared command in silent many item got showed light. Holy Spirit appeared has commanded in silent that this book be named call The New Testament. Holy Spirit appeared command in silent join fight would be breakthrough. Holy Spirit appeared command in silent rice cooker which means Holy God rich bowl.

Holy Spirit appeared command in silent holding an axe sign which means protest. Holy Spirit appeared command in silent fruits which means spiritually fruits. Holy Spirit command in silent wait upon the HOLY LORD for the church. Holy Spirit command in silent spiritually fruits have purpose someone said don't know who. Hearing from the HOLY LORD powerfully abide in his words.

Holy Spirit command in silent provided memory to write how can Holy God harmony of idol. Holy Spirit act in supernaturally way tears weeping cough body swing. Holy Spirit prophesized example hot soup which means problem or sow many new client chosen someone to write testimony hold don't give all happened within a short period of time it true amazed. Holy Spirit command in silent visit mother pray her swollen leg until go back to Holy lord her leg fine. Contribute some money support mother Holy Spirit called in silent hold don't know why few months later go back to LORD.

When preacher preached powerfully strong words and serious abide in bible Holy Spirit tell in silent preacher have Holy Spirit and no running dog. Holy Spirit made body itchy could not sleep wake up online watch sermon act in supernatural way. Pray in tongue for healing spiritually warfare protection or prayer through Holy God with his power welcome Holy Spirit Holy presence supernatural tears flow the truth and the life I am your God.

Holy Spirit command in silent a Chinese bible Matthew scripture 5: 3-10 calendar "Blessed are the poor in spirit, for theirs is the kingdom of heaven. Blessed are those who mourn, for they shall be comforted. Blessed are the meek, for they shall inherit the earth. Blessed are those who hunger and thirst for righteousness, for they shall be filled. Blessed are the merciful, for they shall obtain mercy. Blessed are the pure in heart, for they shall see God. Blessed are the peacemakers, for they shall be called sons of God. Blessed are those who are persecuted for righteousness' sake, for theirs is the kingdom of heaven." Holy Spirit command in silent share sharp.

Holy Spirit command in silent rice bowl which means Holy God. Holy Spirit command in silent the power you know more. Holy Spirit command in silent open wing to fight which means challenging. Holy Spirit command in silent shoot go up mean raise. Holy Spirit appeared command in silent rice cooker which means Holy God rice bowl. Holy

God rice bowl which means Holy God. Holy Spirit appeared command in silent worship the HOLY LORD in daily office hours. Holy Spirit appeared command in silent generation to generation planting new church.

CONCLUSION

God Acts According to
Your Belief in Him

*E*xperience God's kingdom living right now! Experience His dynamic, marvelous, SUPER power in your life! *It's possible; only believe!*

Believe that our Holy God is real and alive in heaven and on earth. Believe that He is a God of miracles, signs and wonders. Believe that with Him all things are possible. Believe that He answers your prayers. Believe that He has a plan for your life and that He directs your destiny.

God Himself commands us to believe in Him:

> And without faith it is impossible to please God, because anyone who comes to him must believe that

he exists and that he rewards those who earnestly seek him.

Hebrews 11:6

Believe in your Heavenly Father. Believe in His presence and in His supernatural power. Believe in His mercy and grace. Believe that He loves and strengthens you. Believe that He leads and guides you. Believe that He saves and protects you.

Believe that He is your Healer. Believe that He blesses you with hope, peace and joy. Believe, and receive holy wisdom, anointing, and all kinds of blessings from God!

Note to the Reader:

We invite you to share your response to the message in this book by writing to us at:
The World Power Testimony Books and Gifts
Email: lee_testimony@hotmail.com

Or visit us at:
http://tiny.cc/lee_gifts
Facebook page: lee_testimony
Testimony link: http://tiny.cc/lee_testimony

www.ingramcontent.com/pod-product-compliance
Lightning Source LLC
Chambersburg PA
CBHW031323040426
42443CB00005B/202